Ac......

Four Wheels
to Freedom

"I was deeply moved by the account that Victor Lerch has created. The author describes so well the atmosphere of such an abnormal time, and he succeeds in identifying with the feelings and experiences of the people he writes about. This book brought me close to Dr. Lerch and his family."

— Margrit Wreschner Rustow, Ravensbrück Survivor

"An extremely engaging account of one family's struggle to survive Hitler's brutal regime. The writer immediately captures your interest and holds it throughout with vivid accounts of heroic acts of ordinary people. These stories, with accompanying photographs of the actual people, create a powerful connection between the reader and the characters. And unlike many other Holocaust works I have read, this book chronicles the experience of an interfaith couple and how this group of Jews who converted from their religion did not escape Nazi terror."

— Donald S. Berger, Head of School, Cary Academy

"A very fluid and personal narrative describing extraordinary acts of survival within Hitler's Germany by the author's seemingly ordinary German / Jewish grandparents. It is a testament to the quiet strength of family and personal integrity as well as to showier acts of bravery. This is one of those quiet books that makes a deep impression."

— Grace Minior, former editor for Houghton Mifflin

FOUR WHEELS TO FREEDOM

A Tale of Survival in Hitler's Germany

VICTOR LERCH

Having My Say
PUBLICATIONS

FOUR WHEELS TO FREEDOM
A Tale of Survival in Hitler's Germany
Copyright © 2009 by Victor Lerch

Having My Say Publications
10204 Clairbourne Place
Raleigh, NC 27615
www.fourwheelstofreedom.com
www.havingmysay.net

Book and cover design by Michael Brechner / Cypress House

Permissions
Every effort has been made to trace the copyright holders of quoted materials in this book. The publisher apologizes for any errors or omissions and would be grateful if notified of any corrections that should be incorporated in future reprints or editions of this book.

Publisher's Cataloging-in-Publication Data

Lerch, Victor.
  Four wheels to freedom : a tale of survival in Hitler's Germany / Victor Lerch. -- 1st ed. -- Raleigh, NC : Having My Say Publications, 2008.
  p. ; cm.
  ISBN: 978-0-9798887-1-7
  Includes bibliographical references.
  1. Germany--History--1933-1945. 2. Jews--Germany--History--1933-1945. 3. Germany--Biography. 4. Courage. I. Title.
  DD256.5 .L47 2008   2007941181
  943.086--dc22 2008

Printed in the USA
4 6 8 9 7 5 3
First edition

In Memory of My Grandparents,
Friedrich and Selma Zins,
The two most extraordinary people I have ever met.

CONTENTS

PROLOGUE

When I was a small boy, my mother seized my imagination with stories of how she and her parents survived both Hitler and the Allied bombings during World War II. They were terrific tales, and ones that I never tired of hearing, but there was one thing that always bothered me. I could never quite figure out how my grandparents, the seemingly mild-mannered pair we all affectionately knew as Nanny and Poppop, could have done the daring things my mother said they did.

Even now, more than twenty years after they've been gone, not a week goes by that I don't think about the two of them. What was it about the character of Friedrich and Selma Zins that enabled them to overcome the mortal dangers they faced? I'm convinced that their lives stand as an example for all of us — a gift to future generations of our family that I want my children to understand. Inevitably, I began to feel my memories of Nanny and Poppop slipping away with the passage of time. My mother senses it too, and we've talked frequently of the need to somehow preserve their legacy. In the years since my grandparents left us, it seemed as if an irreplaceable lesson was in danger of being lost.

From an early age, I could sense that there was something different about these two people. Every summer after school let out, I couldn't wait for my chance to spend a week alone with them, free of the competing demands of my siblings. Each morning, at a quarter to six, Poppop would roust me out of bed in their small apartment in the Bronx where he worked as the building superintendent. Together we would climb the hill in front of the six-story structure at 3111 Heath Avenue,

1

headed for the nearby corner store. Our mission: to return with two identical newspapers. Breakfast was the only time during the day that Nanny and Poppop permitted themselves to relax long enough to read the paper, so each of them had to have their own copy. When the morning meal was over, we boys got up and headed out to do the work around the building, while Nanny wasted no time breaking out her feather duster and tidying their already spotless apartment. At precisely 11:45, we returned for lunch, no matter what. Afterward came more chores, followed by dinner promptly at 5:30. I've always liked my life well ordered, and daily life with Friedrich and Selma Zins was a tightly regimented affair. Even as a child, I loved it.

Sometimes, when I got tired in the afternoons, I would ask my grandfather why he bothered to mop the hallways when everything always seemed so perfectly clean in the first place. "How do you think it got that way?" he replied knowingly, without the slightest trace of anger. I learned from him early on that satisfaction came from a job well done, no matter how mundane the task.

I can still remember the soldierly rows of garbage cans, standing in perfect formation in the entryway of their apartment house, each with its lid squarely in place. Friedrich Zins would permit no unsightly rubbish to protrude, so twice each day he donned his work gloves and shifted the bags from front to back, just to make it easier for his tenants to deposit the new day's discards at the front of the row. The rotting garbage smelled awful to me, of course, but there was such an undeniable comfort in the routine that I couldn't wait until I was old enough to help him. Poppop even gave me my own special pair of work gloves, just like the ones he had.

Then there was the time the boiler broke down. It was an ancient-looking contraption, responsible for supplying all the heat and hot water for the building's several dozen residents. The enormous cauldron squatted in the basement, looking to me like it had been salvaged from some previous life exploring the ocean depths. The landlord had wanted to call in an outside repairman, but Friedrich Zins would have none of it. The way my grandfather saw it, his boss had paid him to do a job and this was something he was pretty certain he could handle. Late one night, after his tenants had all gone to bed, he shut down the furnace and waited. A couple of hours later, when the metal had cooled down enough to touch, Poppop slipped into his coveralls, hoisted himself inside the cavernous chamber, and went to work. I remember making Nanny promise to wake me up that night, so we could keep each other company during the tense couple of hours that he was inside that contraption. Everything turned out fine, but had the furnace accidentally started up again while my grandfather was still inside, he would surely have been badly injured or killed. By the time the residents woke up the next morning, none of them aware of their superintendent's middle-of-the-night escapades, the whole system was functioning normally again. In the years to come, I was to learn that my grandfather was no stranger to taking risks — if he believed the reason was important enough.

As a child, I never thought to ask Poppop if it mattered to him that most of what he did was menial labor, and I never heard him use that as an excuse to give it anything less than his best. He didn't need to explain why, either. His actions spoke for him. When my mother told the stories about him during the war, she never said, "Your grandfather did this because," or "This is the way it should have been done." She didn't have to be that explicit. It was obvious to me, even as a youngster, that for Friedrich Zins there was just a right way and a wrong way to do things. If you took on a job, then you were obligated to do it well.

As I grew older and learned more about how the world worked, the stories I'd first heard as a child fed a burgeoning desire to comprehend the source of my grandparents' great courage. Gradually, during my younger adult years, I developed an unquenchable need to go and live for a while in the land of their birth. At first, I thought that this was just about wanting to experience firsthand the culture of my heritage, but I know now that there was more to it than that. Gradually, as I unearthed the details of my grandparents' lives, my admiration for these two very ordinary people grew ever greater. "What would my grandparents have done?" has come to be my unfaltering standard when faced with the challenges of my own life.

When I started this project, my intent was just to preserve my mother's accounts of her parents' wartime exploits for the generations of our family who will never have the good fortune to have known them in person. But the more I learned about the things that Friedrich and Selma Zins did during the war, the more I wanted to see for myself the places where the critical events in their lives — those dramatic tales I first heard when I was growing up — actually took place. I never imagined then what an incredible journey this would turn out to be.

That search has now stretched across two continents and filled more than a decade of my life. I've sat spellbound, listening to first-hand accounts of the survivors of Ravensbrück, the concentration camp where my grandmother spent sixteen months of her life — horrifying stories that sound unbelievable even now, except for the fact that they are true. I've spent dozens of hours poring over long-forgotten files in dusty old archives, occasionally punctuated by the indescribable thrill of discovering a critical piece of the story buried in some half-century-old document. Together with my mother, I've walked through the concentration camps of Eastern Europe and seen for myself the places where the Nazis murdered my grandmother's entire family, along with so many others. I also visited the village where, having escaped from the camps but still trapped behind Soviet lines, my grandmother stole across the border under cover of darkness, risking everything to get back home again. It was there that I met Christa Bauer, granddaughter of the man who smuggled her to freedom that night more than sixty years ago. I listened as Frau Bauer told me a near-identical version of the escape story that she had heard as a young child from her own grandfather.

Best of all, perhaps, throughout our mutual voyage of discovery, my relationship with my mother has grown and deepened. I'll never forget standing with her on the ruins of the crematoria at Auschwitz-Birkenau, surrounded by a sea of blue and white Stars of David, each adorning one of the tiny flags planted by those who had come to remember. Just being there was painful enough, but hearing my mother talk about the grandparents, aunts, uncles, and cousins she had known as a young girl, most of whom had perished on that very spot, made the reality of their loss almost unbearable. Now, as my mother progresses with infinite grace through her later years, I'm grateful beyond words for the experiences we've had the chance to share.

I think this is a book I've wanted to write for most of my life. I can count on one hand the number of dreams I've had that I can remember, but shortly after moving to Germany in the late 1980s I had one I will never forget. As I lay in bed that night, in our apartment next to the vineyards in a small village north of Heidelberg, I dreamt that I was traveling through the German countryside by train with my mother and a couple of old family friends. As luck would have it, the locomotive broke down, and as the youngest of the bunch, I was the obvious choice to set out on foot to look for help. After walking for a while, I came upon an isolated farmhouse. An old man greeted me at the door, his large straw hat partially pulled down in front, shading most of his face. In a voice both kind and strong, he bid me to come in and pointed to a seat on the sofa. "Wait just a minute, please," the old fellow said, "there's someone I'd like you to meet." A few minutes later, he returned, ushering his wife into the room. I looked up and gasped at the sight of my grandmother standing in front of me. Then the old man reached up and slowly raised the hat from his head, a wry smile arcing toward the so-familiar twinkle in one eye. "Didn't you recognize me?" my grandfather said. "We've been waiting a long time for you to come."

I. BERLIN

Of all of my grandparents' exploits during the war, my favorite story is the one about how my grandfather, a common laborer determined to free his wife from the concentration camp, single-handedly took on the Nazi bureaucracy in the seat of its power. I had heard bits and pieces of this intriguing tale several times as a boy, but never the whole story from start to finish. It was a couple of days after Christmas one year — I was a teenager by then I think — when my mother and I found ourselves with a few unexpected moments alone together. We were sitting on the sofa in my grandparents' tiny apartment, basking in the warmth that pervaded their household every year at holiday time. I begged her to tell me again about her father's quest to Berlin.

It began late in the summer of 1943, and although this is a story mostly about my grandfather, it begins with my grandmother. Selma was at St. Elisabeth's Hospital in Frankfurt, recovering from a hysterectomy, an operation she later described as having been "touch and go." She had taken more than the usual risks in having the surgery. Some years earlier, as part of its systematic campaign of discrimination, the Nazi government had banned Jews from receiving treatment at all public hospitals. Until that time, by virtue of her marriage to an Aryan man, my grandmother had enjoyed some protection from the worst of Hitler's abuses. That didn't help her in this case. Selma and her surgeon, Dr. Rudolph Freisfeld, must have known that they were breaking the law, but they had little choice. After ten years of Nazi rule, no Jewish institution in the city was still capable of performing such major

7

surgery. My grandfather was visiting his wife a few days after the operation when Gestapo agents burst into her room and dragged Selma from her hospital bed.

My grandparents were never quite sure who had tipped off the authorities, though they had their suspicions. Friedrich's brother-in-law, Willi Göbel, told them that the culprit was Maria, the wife of my grandfather's older brother Valentin. Willi, who had earlier joined the SS to further his otherwise dim job prospects, most likely had inside information. Maria Zins wasn't a Nazi sympathizer, just a ruthless opportunist. If she sensed the slightest possibility of personal gain, she would have leapt at the chance to turn my grandmother in — regardless of the pain it might have caused the rest of her family. Most of my grandfather's brothers and sisters, some of whom had had their own bad experiences with their sister-in-law, were convinced of Maria's guilt as well, and those who are still alive continue to echo that indictment to this day.

There was one other possibility, too. Across the street from where my grandparents lived, in the Praunheim section of Frankfurt, sat a row of small family businesses with a dairy store at one end. The wife of the shop owner, Frau Wochele, was an ardent and well-known supporter of Hitler, and she made no effort to conceal her frustration with my grandmother's protected status. Since *Molkereiprodukte Wochele* was the only place within easy walking distance to get milk and cheese, Selma had to shop there, though she complained bitterly about the verbal lashings she regularly received from the proprietress. Eventually, my grandmother grew so tired of the constant abuse that she took to offering the *Heil Hitler!* salute upon entering the store, but even this failed to placate her nemesis. Still, despite Frau Wochele's hatred of all things Jewish, my grandfather never really believed that it was the dairy store owner who had denounced his wife, if for no other reason than had she wanted to she could have done so long before Selma ever went into the hospital. The Nazis had been encouraging citizens to drum up accusations against the Jews for years, and formal evidence was rarely required.

"Selma, with friends, in her hospital bed at the Elizabethenkranken-haus (Note presence of unidentified uniformed man in background)"

And so, despite the fact that Selma was still in her own words "weak and nervous" from the surgery, the Gestapo arrested my grandmother while her husband looked on, powerless to intervene. Because of her condition, my grandmother's captors took her to the so-called *Sammel-haus* ("collection house") located at Hermesweg 5-7, instead of throwing her into the city jail on Hammelsgasse as they did with most Jewish prisoners. Used primarily to house Jews awaiting deportation, part of the Hermesweg facility had also been converted into a small infirmary. The official police documents listed *Rasse* ("race") as the reason for Selma's detention. This was consistent with the assumption that she had been arrested for violating one of the myriad laws restricting Jewish behavior, in this case the prohibition against treatment in public hospitals. With Selma now in custody, my grandparents had no idea when or if she might ever be allowed to return home.

The Nazis allowed my grandfather to come into the *Sammelhaus* once a week to visit his wife and for the next couple of months, nothing much seemed to happen. Then, one afternoon, the event my grandparents had been fearing occurred. Suspiciously, it was Maria who came to my grandparents' apartment to report having seen Nazi guards with their dogs marching Selma through the main train station and loading her into a locked passenger car at the back of a train. Friedrich rushed down to find her, but he was already too late. Before he could get there, Selma was gone. My grandfather returned home and told his daughters simply, "They're taking her."

For weeks afterward, the three of them heard nothing. As the days slowly passed, the waiting grew intolerable, especially since Friedrich was convinced that the Nazis had violated their own laws exempting Jews in mixed marriages when they deported his wife. With time dragging on and no news of Selma's whereabouts, my grandfather decided he had to act. He quickly discovered, however, that he would have to go all the way to Berlin if he hoped to win Selma's release.

Earlier in 1943, Nazi bureaucrats had officially dissolved the *Jüdische Gemeinde*, Frankfurt's Jewish Community organization, and created instead a single agency in charge of the affairs of all Jews remaining in the Reich. The *Restvereinigung der jüdischen Mischehepartner Bezirksstelle der Juden in Deutschland* operated exclusively out of a centralized location in Berlin. Only a skeleton crew remained to oversee local operations in Frankfurt, and no one there had the ability to override Selma's deportation order.

Traveling to Berlin in the midst of a war would be no easy thing. Although non-Jews were still permitted to move about the country at will, government agents were always on the lookout for any unusual behavior. Anyone who veered from the routine risked being picked up for interrogation, or worse. Despite the dangers, Friedrich was unwilling to just sit and wait, hoping that his wife would somehow be all right. He decided to make the trip.

The arrangements proved complicated. My grandfather could not ask for time off from work for an errand like this, and finding the money for the train fare was a problem as well. Cash had always been tight in my grandparents' household, and as the war ground on, the family's economic situation had only deteriorated. Friedrich, a machinist by trade, had been demoted to doing unskilled piecework on the graveyard shift as a result of resisting official pressure to divorce his Jewish wife. My grandfather did his best to frustrate the regime's attempts to punish him, but each time he would become proficient at a particular task and start to earn more money, his supervisors would promptly switch him to a new job. His earnings had suffered accordingly.

There was also the problem of leaving his two daughters behind. The Allied bombings were becoming more frequent, and my mother and her sister would have to stay by themselves for at least two nights while he was away. It was true that Erika and Inge, at ages twelve and ten by then, had become quite used to fending for themselves in the weeks since their mother had gone. But their father would now be much too far away to help if one of them got hurt or the Gestapo came calling. There was also the chance that my grandfather might not return at all. What if the authorities took offense at his demands, and decided to lock him up or deport him to the camps too? What would happen to his girls then? Still, in spite of all the reasons he could think of not to make the trip, Friedrich knew he had to try. He arranged for his brother Heinrich, who lived nearby, to look in on Erika and Inge once or twice while he was gone, but for the most part the girls would be on their own.

A few days later, my grandfather came home from work one morning, grabbed a few hours' sleep, then got up and packed himself some food for the trip. As evening approached, he kissed his daughters goodbye and set out on foot for the main station, where he bought himself a ticket on the express train headed east. Climbing on board, he curled himself uncomfortably into the second-class seat, trying to ignore the thoughts racing around in his head and get some rest. He arrived in Berlin very early in the morning after a fitful night's sleep that left him

FOUR WHEELS TO FREEDOM

feeling fatigued and hung-over. As Friedrich left the station, the scene in the German capital must have astonished him. By late 1943, the Allies had struck Berlin relentlessly, and nothing that Frankfurt had yet suffered could compare to the devastation my grandfather now saw around him. Since he was due back at work the following evening, time was short. He shook off his disorientation and set out in search of the offices of the *Restvereinigung*, winding his way circuitously through the unfamiliar rubble-strewn streets.

I'm sure my grandfather had had visions of storming in the front door of the building and going straight to the top man, but I doubt he ever got close to anyone with any real authority. More likely, a low-level functionary wound up dealing with the quixotic little man from Frankfurt. He stated his case and was met with complete disbelief. Had he really come all the way from Frankfurt on such a hopeless mission? Didn't he realize that by making such a demand he was putting himself at risk of deportation as well? Wouldn't it really be better for him if he just divorced his wife now that she had been taken away? And what of the children he had left behind?

Though Friedrich must have realized early on that his mission was not going to succeed, he refused to give up easily, convinced as he was that Selma had been detained unlawfully. In the end, he simply would not leave until the staff of the *Restvereinigung* threatened to call the police and have him arrested on the spot. Finally, Friedrich relented and left the building, trudging back through the bombed-out streets, alone with his thoughts. His quest had sustained him, but with all hope now gone, the stress of the past several weeks consumed him. Exhausted, he arrived back in Frankfurt the next morning and walked home. His daughters, who had not been threatened during his absence, rushed to greet their father at the door. They pumped him for news, but he had nothing good to tell them.

In recent years, I've given a lot of thought to my grandfather's seemingly hopeless quest. I never got the chance to ask him whether he realized at the time how much danger he'd put himself and his daughters in, and whether it would have made any difference to him if he had. I can't help feeling that the whole episode was more than a little bit reckless, and I'm not sure I would have done the same thing in his place. Still, there is something undeniably heroic about what he did, all the more so if he knew how heavily the odds were stacked against him. It had to have been an agonizing choice for him, to leave his daughters behind and unguarded to try to rescue his wife. The fact that Friedrich decided to go to Berlin anyway demonstrated just how strongly he felt that his wife had been wronged. Maybe he just felt that he had no real choice, but I don't think that diminishes the courageous nature of his actions in the least. My grandfather always had a strong sense of right and wrong, and he had long since passed the point where he was willing to sit idly by. In the end, I think that for Friedrich Zins, there simply came a time when he had to do what he thought was right regardless of the consequences. He knew that if his wife were ever to regain her freedom, he was the only chance she had.

II. Beginnings

My grandfather came of age in the working-class district of Bockenheim, just west of the city center of Frankfurt. Today, small mom-and-pop businesses still line the main thoroughfare of Leipziger Strasse. On a quiet side street, a couple of blocks to the south, stands the house where my great-grandparents, Heinrich and Maria Zins, raised their large family in a cramped, three-room apartment. The Zinses were a boisterous and friendly group, none more so than my grandfather, third youngest of the eight siblings. Handsome and athletic, Friedel, as he was known to his friends, was a sharp dresser with an outgoing personality.

As a child, Friedel was also an avid prankster who jousted occasionally with the local authorities. More often than not though, with a hint of the determination that would later characterize his adult life, he would find a way to wiggle free of whatever predicament he had stumbled into. My mother loves to tell the story about the day of the fish fight in the schoolyard. No one would say exactly how it all started, of course, but one day after class, my grandfather and his buddies somehow got their hands on a barrel full of fish. Soon thereafter, a battle commenced, with both sides hurling herring at each other until heads, tails and fins of every size and shape littered the playground. After the ammunition ran out and the conflict ended, the headmaster summoned the instigators to his office for an explanation. I like to imagine that, far from being angry, the poor man had a hard time stifling a few laughs of his own. Friedel Zins was mischievous, it was true, but his pranks were never malicious or destructive, and he had the kind of fun-loving personality that made it hard even for those in authority to stay mad at him. Even in his later years when I knew him, my grandfather still had an impossible-to-miss twinkle in the eye, hinting at an enthusiasm for life that spilled over into everything he did.

"Zins family portrait (Friedrich, front row, second from left)"

On another memorable afternoon, Friedel and his friends staged their own version of "Cowboys and Indians" on the grounds of a local cemetery where they liked to play. Some of the boys hid behind the gravestones, others perched themselves high up in trees, waiting to ambush their unsuspecting opponents. Before long, however, the local constabulary got wind of what was going on and sent a posse to break things up. After flushing the boys from their treetop outposts, the police hauled the lot of them down to the station for a little light interrogation. Some of the officers thought it odd that the boys had picked a graveyard to act out their imaginary drama, and in due course they summoned a psychologist to interview the miscreants. To Friedel this was ridiculous. Hoping to make the doctor go away sooner, my grandfather gave the man exactly what he was looking for. Friedel was particularly creative, according to my mother, at inventing crazy-sounding answers for the inkblot test. Given the trouble he was in, this strikes me as rather gutsy, but it was also entirely in character for a man who approached life without fear.

In the end, Friedel's luck held, though not without a little outside assistance. It just so happened that my grandfather's aborted version of the Gunfight at the OK Corral had taken place on the Kaiser's birthday, and, in his own honor, the king decided to pardon all minor offenders across the country that day. This fortunate decree also extended to all underage trespassing cowboys, even those who, like Friedel, were happily unrepentant.

Owing in part to the large number of mouths to feed, my grandfather's family had never been especially well off. Nevertheless, his parents always welcomed others into their home warmly, and Heinrich and Maria Zins also encouraged their children to bring their friends along to the family get-togethers they regularly held. Emmi, the youngest of the eight siblings, sometimes invited her favorite schoolmate, a young Jewish girl named Selma Schwanthaler, and before long Friedel was introduced to his little sister's best friend. It's hard to know now what the dashing Friedel saw in the shy and poorly dressed Selma, but I like to think that perhaps he sensed the strength of character hidden beneath her plain appearance. Whatever the source of their mutual attraction, my grandparents began a courtship that culminated in their marriage on January 31, 1931.

Selma's upbringing had been quite a bit different. This was mostly the result of the choices that her own mother, Jenny, had made as a younger woman. Jenny Löwenthal had been born to a prosperous and up-and-coming Jewish couple in June 1880, at a time of great optimism for Jews in Germany. In Frankfurt especially, where they made up fully 5 percent of the city's population (five times higher than in the country as a whole) Jews had achieved a level of social and geographic integration within the wider community that was unprecedented in the history of Europe. As the 20th century approached, many Jewish families had migrated out of the traditional neighborhoods in the eastern part of the city, choosing instead to settle among their non-Jewish counterparts in more affluent sections of Frankfurt. Though they were never quite accepted as equals, Frankfurt's Jews were active in all aspects of community life, and the city owed its prosperity in no small part to the contributions of its Jewish citizens. Second only to the capital of Berlin, Frankfurt in the early 1900s had gained a reputation as the "Jewish Metropolis."

"Best of friends, Selma and Emmi"

As a young girl, Selma's mother had been persistently willful and impulsive. Among other things, Jenny found it difficult to accept Orthodox Judaism's view of women as unequal and subservient, an attitude that clashed frequently with the devout brand of Judaism practiced by the rest of her family. Jenny's behavior often shocked her parents, but she was far from alone in her progressive views. By the time she reached her teenage years, increasing numbers of Jews had chosen to shed the old ways in hopes of better assimilating into the community around them. This trend had broad societal implications as well. Most Jews living in Germany had come to see their country of residence as their only true homeland, leaving them (ironically as it later turned out) with little need to support the establishment of a separate state of their own. As a result, the Zionism gaining popularity in Eastern Europe during this same time was largely absent from Germany.

After a tumultuous childhood and against the wishes of her parents, Jenny left home at age twenty-three to marry one Karl Gustav Schwanthaler, presumably for love. Jenny's new husband had also come from a relatively well-off Jewish family, but at the time the two met, he was making an undistinguished living as an office worker. Even though Karl Schwanthaler was, like Jenny's father, a fellow Bavarian, he could not convince the Löwenthals that he was good enough for their daughter. Empowered by his economic success, Jonas Löwenthal had long harbored aspirations of someday joining the privileged echelons of Frankfurt's upper classes. Despite his frequent disagreements with his independent-minded daughter, he had hoped she would have the sense to choose a better match.

Jenny went ahead with her plans anyway, and after the wedding her parents cut off all contact with their daughter and her new husband. Most of Jenny's siblings followed suit, creating an unbridgeable rift between Jenny and her family that was to persist for decades.

It's hard now to imagine how Jenny's choice to marry against her parents' wishes could have produced such lasting divisions, and I can't help thinking there must have been more to the story. Perhaps Jenny's parents also ostracized her for a perceived lack of devotion to Judaism. Even today, many Orthodox Jews look down with contempt at those whom they view as less than adequately observant. There could have been other reasons too, but, with the principals all long since dead and no one left to ask, it's impossible to know what else might have divided the Löwenthals. Worse yet, none of them could have foreseen the repercussions that would flow from this falling-out years later. What began as a source of disappointment and regret for Jenny and her family would eventually have tragic consequences when the Nazis came to power.

"Karl Gustav Schwanthaler, father of Selma Zins
(standing at right)"

Jenny and her first husband had two children. Bertha, born in October 1904, inherited much of her mother's impulsiveness, but without the moderating influence of Jenny's innate intelligence. As a result, her behavior often bordered on the reckless. Selma, my grandmother, arrived almost exactly three years later. In contrast to her sister, the Schwanthalers' second daughter was shy and studious, with a natural reluctance to take chances and a preference for always thinking things through before acting. As a child, Selma was also quite frail physically, a problem made worse by her poor eyesight and a marked tendency toward clumsiness.

Despite her outward handicaps, however, my grandmother turned out to have a much more important gift. Hidden deep below the surface, where it took many years to become apparent, she had also inherited her mother's unshakable will.

Selma's early life was difficult. Her parents struggled to put food on the table, and the young family moved almost yearly through a series of apartments in Frankfurt until February 1911, when disaster struck. With his youngest daughter only a little more than three years old, Karl Schwanthaler died suddenly of tuberculosis. After the funeral, Jenny tried her best to earn a living as a dressmaker, but she was unable to take in enough work to support her two small children. By late April, scarcely two months after her husband's death, she had no choice but to break up the family. Reluctantly, Jenny delivered Bertha to the *Israelitische Waisenhaus*, a local orphanage operated by the Jewish Community of Frankfurt. At least she was able to keep Selma with her.

Several months later, still struggling to get by, Jenny met Berthold Baer, a proud Jewish man with a pronounced streak of Prussian nastiness. Life had not been kind to Berthold either. Hampered by a congenital deformity of one hand, he eked out his meager living as a shoemaker. To a desperate Jenny, though, a union with Berthold offered the possibility of reuniting her shattered family. The couple married on February 25, 1914, by which time Jenny was already two months pregnant with their first child. Not long afterward, Jenny retrieved Bertha from the orphanage, bringing her eldest daughter home to join the rest of the reconstructed family.

By August, the new baby, whom they named Hermann, had arrived. In December of the following year a second child, a girl this time, came to Jenny and Berthold. Sadly, little Rosa Baer would die from malnutrition before her third birthday, a victim of both the deprivations of World War I and her own family's increasingly precarious finances. Her tiny grave can still be found in a shady corner of the Jewish Cemetery (*Jüdischer Friedhof*) on Rat-Beil-Strasse in Frankfurt.

*"At work—Jenny and Berthold in the shoemaker's shop
(note congenital deformity of Berthold's right hand)"*

Selma's adolescent years didn't get much happier. Berthold doted
on his only son, but he treated his stepdaughters harshly. At one point
there had been talk of sending Selma to college, but with more mouths
to feed and never enough money to go around, tuition fell impossibly
beyond her parents' reach. Rather than being the first in her family to go
to university, my grandmother trained as a secretary and went to work
immediately after graduating high school, just as her less gifted sister
had done before her. To keep the household afloat, Berthold confiscated
most of his stepdaughters earnings, leaving little or nothing for the girls
themselves. Much later on, Selma exercised a bit of that iron will she
had inherited and accepted her future in-laws' offer to leave home and
move in with them. Leaving her family before being married was no
small matter for a woman in that place and time, but it was an indica-
tion of just how desperate Selma was to escape her stepfather's tyranny.

"The young couple"

At the time she married Friedel, Selma formally resigned from the Jewish Community of Frankfurt and converted to Lutheranism, the religion of her new husband. My grandparents wanted their children to grow up sharing a single faith, and, like her own mother before her, Selma felt no overwhelming attachment to Judaism. It was a choice she never regretted. Though she could not have known it at the time, my grandmother's decision to convert would later prove critical to her own survival. A decade afterward, when the Nazis began deporting Jews to the concentration camps, they used the Jewish Community's own membership lists as their primary means of identifying their victims. Though classified by the regime as Jewish based on her birth, Selma's name no longer appeared on any official records. Because of this, she escaped the attention of the authorities for years, even as the Nazis relentlessly pursued her fellow Jews.

My grandparents began their lives together in a tiny apartment at Heimatring 4, close to several of Friedel's siblings. Erika, my mother, was born in December of 1931. Her sister, Ingeborg, arrived just sixteen months later. Even though Friedrich and Selma were not especially religious, they decided to have their daughters baptized, and this also turned out to be a fortunate choice. Though Erika and Inge were also officially classified as Jewish under Nazi law (by virtue of their having had a Jewish mother), their parents' decision to raise them in the church meant that the girls' names never appeared on the Jewish Community's membership lists either.

My grandparents ran a strict household. Even as a young father, Friedel believed strongly that there was a right way and a wrong way of doing things, and he was convinced that he knew what the right way should be. Friedel and Selma were especially adamant about maintaining the peace of the family dinner table; their daughters were to be seen and not heard during meals together, and any necessary trips to the bathroom had to be made before they all came to the table. Though the family was not usually in danger of going hungry, at least before the war years, there was never any extra food to waste. In Friedel and Selma's home, children were not permitted to leave the table until they had finished every last morsel on their plates, whether they liked what their mother had put in front of them that night or not.

My grandparents had another hard and fast rule: their daughters were never to speak poorly of others. One Sunday morning, my mother learned this lesson the hard way. It was getting late, and Erika was lounging about in her parents' bed, a treat the girls were permitted only on weekends. A young girl from the neighborhood came calling for her at the front door. It wasn't a child my mother liked very well, and in any case, she was in no mood to get dressed right away and go out and play.

Instead of politely declining, however, Erika belittled her erstwhile play-mate, remarks that earned her an embarrassing tongue-lashing from her father. The fact that it had been just another child that Erika had been rude to mattered to my grandfather not one bit.

"Christmas 1932 with baby Erika at the Zins' house
(note pregnant Selma at right)"

Though Friedel was the stronger disciplinarian of the two, Selma was no slouch either. In order that the few nice things they had might last for the entire week, she expected the girls to change out of their school clothes immediately after arriving home in the afternoon. Not only that, but all their dirty clothes had to be carefully turned right side out before they were put in the laundry. If my mother or her sister broke one of the many household rules, Selma didn't bother to punish them herself. She had a much better weapon than that. "Wait till your father gets home," was a phrase that would set Erika and Inge worrying all afternoon about whether they were in for it when their father found out what they had done. Even if he just scolded them, my grandfather's verbal lashings could be so harsh at times that Erika sometimes preferred a spanking as the less painful of the possible punishments.

Personal responsibility went hand in hand with the strict discipline. The girls each had their specific duties to keep the household running, including cutting up newspapers into small pieces to use as toilet paper and, even when they were very young, emptying their own chamber pots each morning. Erika's parents expected her, as the older of the two, to look out for her little sister, and my grandparents would blame her if they heard about anyone picking on Inge. Still, with all the responsibilities came certain freedoms too. Selma encouraged the girls to read whatever they could get their hands on, a stance that occasionally drew criticism from some of the less open-minded members of my grandfather's family. Ignoring her skeptical in-laws, my grandmother believed firmly that her daughters should be exposed to all kinds of ideas — that far from being harmed by new thinking, this was the best way for them to learn to sort out the good from the bad for themselves.

In spite of all the rules, affection reigned supreme in my grandparents' home. Christmas was always the most special of times. On Christmas Eve, traditionally the time in Germany when children received their gifts, my mother and her sister would willingly trot off to their room for an afternoon nap to insure they would be able to stay awake for the festivities later that night. Most years, my grandparents only had enough money for a couple of new gifts, so, to heighten the suspense for their daughters, they would bring out certain toys only during the holidays. Erika and Inge anticipated these prizes from years past as eagerly as they did their new gifts, all the more so since they already knew what was coming. Their parents would strategically scatter the old favorites in among the newly wrapped gifts, just so that the girls could have the pleasure of "discovering" them anew. After a couple of weeks, Friedel and Selma would gather up the special things and hide them away, waiting to be revealed again at some future Christmas.

II. BEGINNINGS

By 1934, with two toddlers in tow and in dire need of more space, my grandparents moved their young family into a newly constructed apartment building in Praunheim, at what was then the extreme western edge of the city. These modern flats boasted all the latest amenities and were in great demand among working-class couples. The family initially took up residence in the only apartment that was available, a unit up on the second floor. Four years later a ground floor flat opened up, and Friedel and Selma quickly snapped it up. Units on the bottom level included the coveted addition of a small backyard, accessed through a short passageway leading out from the rear of the apartment. This back hallway, which my grandparents dubbed "The Veranda," would later play an important role as a hiding place for Selma's Jewish relatives during the war.

When the Zins girls were old enough, they enrolled at the nearby *Ebelfeldschule*, opened in 1930 specifically to serve the children of families in the new development. At its founding, the school's faculty had adopted the *Frankfurter Lehrplan*, a reform-minded curriculum that emphasized independent thinking on the part of the students and offered teachers wide discretion in choice of subject matter. This would have suited Selma's own philosophy quite well, but by the time my mother and her sister enrolled, the Nazis had already taken power and forced radical changes in the teaching philosophy. One of Erika's teachers, a Herr Brodt, took to the new ideology with particular gusto, instructing his young charges in the proper performance of the Nazi salute and delighting himself by intimidating the students with anti-Semitic stories. Many of Herr Brodt's colleagues, in contrast, preferred to remain as inconspicuous as possible, offering only a half-hearted *Heil Hitler!* salute — and then only when they thought someone else might be watching. A few brave souls, unable to refrain from ridiculing the more outlandish propaganda spewing from the regime, resisted more openly. One teacher even invented his own parody of Nazi sympathizers — saluting awkwardly by bringing his arm up as if attempting to swat a fly from his ear — a performance that routinely elicited laughter from his students. For the most part, however, those who opposed the Nazi order quickly learned that it was much better to keep their opinions to themselves.

"Classroom at the Ebelfeldschule ca. 1935"

My grandparents did their best to shield their daughters from what was going on around them, but slowly Erika and Inge began to sense that things were changing. When my mother reached the requisite age, her parents enrolled her in the local chapter of the Hitler Youth. It wasn't something they wanted to do, but membership was mandatory for all children, and objecting would only have drawn unwanted attention to the family. Even so, it didn't take long for those in charge of the group to learn of Erika's mixed parentage, and they quickly dismissed her because of it. The Hitler Youth incident made my grandparents much more cautious, and they often reminded the girls that discussing their background with anyone outside the immediate family could get them all in serious trouble.

Because of the fact that Selma was Jewish, the relationship between my grandparents and the rest of the Zins family gradually began to deteriorate. While none of Friedel's brothers and sisters were openly anti-Semitic, many of them grew increasingly nervous about the idea of having a Jew in their midst. Most felt (with good reason) that their association with Selma might somehow contaminate them in the eyes of the regime, a chance that few were willing to take. Under the spreading mantle of fear and cowardice induced by the Nazis, many of Friedel's siblings gradually distanced themselves from their "unfortunate" brother and his Jewish wife.

"Erika (second from left) with her Zins first cousins in front of their grandparents' apartment" and . . .

". . . sixty years later with the author's children"

There was one notable exception: my grandfather's older brother, Heinrich. Heinrich Zins, who also happened to live in the same housing complex in Praunheim, was a Socialist by ideology and had little tolerance for the Nazis and their policies. He was easily the family's most outspoken critic of the regime, and on one occasion even spent a few nights in jail for voicing his opinions a bit too openly. On that occasion, when the Gestapo had called him in for questioning, Heinrich decided to take his only son Robert with him, hoping that the presence of a child might encourage his interrogators to be more lenient. The ploy apparently worked, and Heinrich was released a few days later — even as many others who were equally outspoken received far harsher punishments. Heinrich did his best to be a bit more careful after that, attempting (often unsuccessfully) to speak his mind only within the safe confines of family gatherings. Still, there were some things he would not compromise on. Heinrich refused to let his own son join the Hitler Youth or to wear the trademark brown shirt and shorts. As punishment, the Nazis forced young Robert to attend an extra day of school each week, which struck the boy's father as a small price to pay for maintaining his principles. Heinrich Zins was a man of honor, and he alone remained steadfast in his support of his little brother's family throughout the war.

"Friedel's brother Heinrich — a man of honor"

Perhaps not surprisingly, my grandparents felt especially close to Heinrich and his wife Rosel, and to Rosel's brother Otto Kutscher and his wife, Paula, who also lived nearby. The

Kutschers' daughters were nearly the same ages as Erika and Inge, and almost every Sunday during the warmer months, the three families would pack a picnic basket and pedal their bicycles to the nearby Taunus Mountains to spend the day together. (Much later, after Selma escaped from the concentration camp, Paula Kutscher would play a critical role in bringing her old friend back home to her family in Frankfurt).

"In the Taunus mountains, Selma and daughters,
with Heinrich, Rosel, and son Robert"

Although Friedel didn't like it when his siblings treated him so coldly, he could understand their fear. It could have been much worse. To her credit, his mother Maria, as matriarch, never let the rest of the bunch stray too far over the line. She repeatedly ignored appeals to exclude Friedel and his family from the clan's weekly gatherings, and she made it quite clear to all that her son and his Jewish wife were as welcome as ever in her home. *Oma* Maria simply would not tolerate rude treatment of family members in her presence.

31

Though she does not remember feeling threatened herself at the time, my mother does recall sensing that Selma's being Jewish had set their family apart in some important way. The Zins girls had no reason to think that their mother was in any immediate danger either, but it was obvious to both of them that the rest of Selma's relatives were fearful. On several occasions, my mother overheard her grandparents, Jenny and Berthold Baer, talking about the need to "be careful" out on the streets. At the time, she thought that the adults were just being over-cautious, but she would soon find out that they were not exaggerating.

Erika was at school one day when one of her classmates rushed up and stuck a finger in her face, shouting, "Your mother has a Jewish nose!" At the time, she wasn't sure what this meant (most likely her little assailant didn't really know either), though even now my mother can recall how uncomfortable she felt at being singled out in that fashion. Erika was a quiet child by nature, and her first impulse was to let the incident pass in the hopes that not too many of her classmates had noticed. That didn't sit very well with her best friend, Friedel Gallinat, however. Friedel wasn't Jewish herself, but as a big girl for her age she had endured more than her own fair share of taunting from the other children, and she was not one to suffer in silence. Quickly, Friedel devised a plan for revenge.

My grandparents could only afford to give their daughters enough money for trolley fare one way each day, so the girls usually rode the streetcar in the morning and walked home in the afternoon when it was warmer and they were in less of a rush. Along the way, on one side of the Hindenburgstrasse, the main avenue between school and home, stood a large brick factory at the bottom of a steep hill. A thick hedge ran along the top of the slope, fronted by a low guardrail. To allay any suspicions on the part of their intended victim, Erika and Friedel bided their time for a few days. When they could wait no longer, the two friends hid themselves in the bushes at the side of the road after school and waited. As Erika's assailant came strolling by, the two friends burst out of the hedge together and shoved their classmate over the guardrail. The little girl propellered her way over and over down the hill, until at last she came to a stop in a dusty heap at the bottom, her belongings scattered in a wide arc. No serious harm had been done, but the message got through loud and clear. No one at school ever bothered Erika about being Jewish again. Revenge had been sweet, but my mother had also gotten her first small taste of just what it meant to be Jewish in Hitler's Germany.

"Ebelfeldschule *and brick factory ca. 1930
(Note Taunus mountains in background)*"

III. KRISTALLNACHT

In January 1933, just two years after my grandparents had begun their lives together, Adolf Hitler seized power in Germany. Capitalizing on a growing sense of popular discontent, the new regime focused blame for the country's ills on the Jews and other minorities. Hitler and his men moved quickly to intensify persecution of the Reich's "impure" citizens, beginning with a general boycott of all Jewish businesses. Though widely ignored at first by a population not yet cowed by Nazi authority, the ban gradually succeeded in depriving many Jews of their livelihoods. In a series of additional steps from April to October 1933, the Nazi government barred Jews from all civil service jobs and professional practices, prohibited their attendance at public places, eliminated all access to higher education, and outlawed ownership of personal possessions such as radios, telephones and, later, even woolen clothing. Shocked and unnerved by the rapidity of events, many Jews retreated into the relative safety of their own homes and increasingly avoided being seen in public.

On September 15, 1935, the Nazi party pushed through a new set of edicts, formally stripping the Jews and other undesirables of their rights of citizenship. The infamous *Nuremberg Gesetze* created multiple groups of individuals, each of which was entitled to a different set of rights. By virtue of having four Jewish grandparents, the new laws classified my grandmother, as *Volljuden* ("fully Jewish"), part of a group subjected to the full brunt of the regime's discriminatory practices. Fortunately for Selma, her status as the wife of a non-Jew secured her a temporary reprieve from the worst of the Nazis' excesses. This may seem to modern observers to have been an odd instance of restraint, but at the time, German society viewed the family unit as sacrosanct. Even Adolf Hitler, as powerful as he was becoming, was hesitant to alienate members of his Aryan constituency by interfering in their marriages.

My mother and her sister officially became *Mischlinge* (literally — "mixed breeds"), and it was here that my grandparents' earlier decision to raise their girls as Lutherans (made for other reasons at the time) turned out to be critical. The minority of *Mischlinge* who were members of the Jewish Community endured the full wrath of the regime, no different from the *Volljuden*. The rest, like Erika and Inge, got to keep their rights of citizenship — at least initially. Nevertheless, in spite of their temporary good fortune, all *Mischlinge* lived in constant fear that the regime could do away with their privileged status at any moment.

The *Nuremberg Gesetze* also prohibited sexual contact or marriage between Jews and other Germans, with violators subject to imprisonment and/or deportation. Fortunately for my grandparents, the Nazis chose not to enforce this particular provision against mixed religious couples who were already living together. This was no small matter. At the time the new laws were enacted, as many as 50,000 people, or more than one in ten Jews living in Germany, were married to non-Jewish partners. Although the Gestapo enjoyed calling in German spouses for occasional "consultations," they stopped short of forcibly nullifying existing marriages. Instead, Nazi officers usually limited themselves to giving friendly "advice," sessions that sometimes ended with threats of job loss or even imprisonment for one's continued refusal to abandon a Jewish mate.

Government officials often pressured the non-Jewish spouses with an awful choice. The regime would agree to exempt permanently their mixed-breed children from persecution, but only at the cost of consenting to an immediate divorce, an act that would invariably doom the Jewish partner. In 1938, the National Marriage Act added additional inducements.

After that, non-Jews could dissolve their unions on the spot, simply by admitting that they now saw their earlier decision to marry a Jew as a mistake. My grandfather, like the majority of Germans in mixed marriages, never gave this a second thought. In spite of the mounting pressure, Friedel refused to deliver his wife to the hands of the regime.

Individual Jews responded to the increasingly oppressive conditions in widely differing ways. The vast majority simply could not accept the new reality—that living in peace in their own country was no longer an option. Despite the obvious and growing danger, most Jews clung to the hope that the Nazi party's dominance would be short-lived and that their lives would eventually return to normal. The alternative—leaving behind the lives and communities they had built and starting over from scratch in a foreign land—seemed too drastic a solution. A prescient few, especially those who were younger or less fearful of beginning anew, became convinced that there was no future for them in Germany. My grandparents, who were starting to feel the effects of Nazi persecution but remained protected from the worst excesses, found themselves somewhere in the middle.

In the early years of Hitler's rule, it was lack of economic opportunity, rather than fear of bodily harm, that energized Jewish emigration. This was very much by design. The Nazis used their multiple boycotts and pronouncements to push the Jews into leaving the country "voluntarily." My grandfather understood that his job prospects would be increasingly limited if he chose to stay married to his Jewish wife. He became convinced that the longer they all remained in Germany, the more his ability to support his family would be at risk. Earlier in their marriage, even before the Nazis codified their persecution of the Jews into law, my grandparents had speculated about immigrating to the United States in search of a better life. The passage of the *Nuremberg Gesetze* finally spurred them to action, but by then it was already too late. They applied for visas to enter the US, but received quota numbers that were hopelessly far down the list. Lacking the money to bribe their way up, Friedel and Selma resigned themselves to a lengthy wait. Instead, it was my grandmother's half-brother, Hermann, who became the first in the family with a chance to escape.

As a newly minted but fully Jewish engineer, Hermann knew he had no chance of finding work as long as Hitler was in power. He had applied for and been granted a visa to enter Argentina, a country far easier to get into than the US, and one which by the mid-1930s already boasted a sizeable contingent of expatriate Germans. Still, Hermann felt pushed into making a move he was not ready for. Although life for the Jews had grown increasingly uncomfortable, acts of violence were still infrequent and the horrible realities of the Final Solution remained inconceivable. Hermann was well aware how difficult it was to obtain a visa to emigrate, and he knew that the opportunity to escape might not come again, but by going to South America, he was leaving behind everything that mattered to him. In addition, he had no idea when or if he might ever see any of his loved ones again.

On July 18, 1935, Hermann traveled to the Port of Hamburg and boarded the passenger ship *Vigo*, bound for Buenos Aires. En route, as the ship crossed the equator, crew members held the traditional ceremony inducting first-time travelers into the Neptune Society. It was intended to be a comical affair, but Hermann's mood was anything but lighthearted. At the climax of the proceedings, Hermann received a certificate bearing his official new title of "*Seebär*" — a whimsical play on his family name — but the attempt at humor only made him feel even more homesick.

After more than a month at sea, the reluctant Hermann and his fellow refugees arrived at their destination. He knew immediately that he could not stay. It took a few days to re-provision the ship for its return voyage, and when the *Vigo* set sail for Germany a week later, Hermann Baer was once again onboard. After docking back in Hamburg on September 20, Hermann slunk back to Frankfurt, unsure what sort of welcome his lack of courage would produce from friends and relatives. A few days after arriving home, trying to raise his spirits a bit, he decided to attend a singles dance sponsored by the Jewish Community. There, for the first time, he met a young woman by the name of Rosi Eckstein.

"The reluctant emigré Hermann Baer"

Rosi had come to Frankfurt from the tiny hamlet of Altenstadt, out in the surrounding countryside. She had left home several years earlier to train for a career in sales, before eventually finding her way to the city in search of a job. By the time Rosi arrived in Frankfurt, however, the Nazi boycott was already in full force and there was no chance for a young Jewish girl to find employment in the regular economy. She signed on instead as a live-in housekeeper for the Wertheims, one of the city's wealthier Jewish families.

Even in the small rural town where she grew up, Rosi had experienced the Nazi threat first hand. Local police had arrested her uncle and his family on trumped-up charges and paraded them in chains through the streets in full view of their friends and neighbors. On another occasion, local youths had vandalized the small Jewish cemetery at the edge of town, smashing centuries-old headstones and trampling on the graves with impunity. Rosi's parents, Wilhelm and Pauline Eckstein, had also personally felt the effects of Nazi persecution as the regime's boycott had squeezed the income of the family's butcher store. As the months ground on, the Ecksteins had begun talking openly about the day that they would have to shut down their business and abandon their home.

Right from the beginning of their two-year courtship, Hermann and Rosi began planning for the day that they would leave Germany together. Decades later, when I talked with my Aunt Rosi about this time in her life, I told her how much I admired her courage in making such a difficult choice, but she quickly dismissed my compliments. "There was no decision to make," Rosi told me. There had been no future for them as Jews in Germany, economically or otherwise, she said. "Leaving was the only thing that would keep us alive."

Despite her protestations to the contrary, I don't think Rosi is giving herself enough credit. No doubt it helped that Hermann and Rosi had seen the example of others around them who had successfully escaped, but it is also true that many of their friends and relatives, faced with exactly the same set of circumstances, failed to find the strength to act as decisively. Rosi's own brother and sister, Julius and Irma Eckstein, had already fled to the US, and she would have gone with them if it had not been for her burgeoning relationship with Hermann. Rosi also watched as the family she worked for bribed their way out, using their wealth to move to the front of the visa line. The Wertheims eventually landed in Mexico, although most of their possessions, including a cache of diamonds they had hidden in a sofa, were "diverted" en route and never seen again.

III. KRISTALLNACHT

In order to escape from Germany, Jewish émigrés needed both an entry visa and a substantial wad of cash. The amounts varied by destination, with the US having by far the most stringent requirements. To assure that they would be self-supporting, anyone who wanted to enter the United States had to be able to prove a minimum of $10,000 in personal assets, the equivalent of almost $140,000 in today's dollars. For the vast majority who could not hope to amass such a sum, the only alternative was to obtain an affidavit of sponsorship from a private individual or charitable organization. Would-be refugees also needed additional funds to pay for the cost of the voyage itself. For most Jews, increasing numbers of whom were unemployed in Hitler's Germany, even these smaller amounts represented an insurmountable barrier.

Obtaining the entry visa was an uphill battle as well. Most countries had strict limits on the numbers of Nazi refugees they would accept, and this was especially true of a United States of America still mired in the effects of the Great Depression. To make matters worse, Jews from Frankfurt who wanted to enter the US had to apply through the American Consulate in Stuttgart, where the quota system was widely known to be corrupt. Anyone with the money to offer a large enough bribe could move to the front of the line, meaning that their less well-off brethren, including my grandparents and all their relatives, kept getting pushed further and further down the list.

Hermann and Rosi had no chance of accumulating the amount of money they needed to satisfy US officials, so they began to look for a sponsor. They pleaded with Hermann's Uncle Morris, who had settled in the US decades earlier. Despite being comfortable financially, Morris Baer was reluctant to make the commitment for fear of having to support the couple indefinitely. With no other viable alternatives, however, Hermann and Rosi kept up the pressure, and Uncle Morris, realizing that his niece and nephew had no one else to turn to, eventually agreed.

Hermann and Rosi knew that their time was running out. Even before they were married in June of 1938, Rosi had begun selling the couple's furniture and other belongings, trying to raise enough money for their passage to America. Even with Uncle Morris' backing, the wait for their visas was taking much too long. Every day, near the couple's apartment on Martin-Luther-Strasse in a predominantly non-Jewish section of northeastern Frankfurt, jack-booted SS troops goose-stepped their way along the wide avenue, chanting: *"Ja, und wenn Judenblut am Messer spritzt, ei, dann geht's noch mal so gut* (Yes, and when Jewish blood sprays upon the knife, oh, then everything will once again be fine)."

By the fall of 1937, the Nazis had finally forced Rosi's parents to close down their butcher shop in Altenstadt. With no way to support themselves, Wilhelm and Pauline decided to sell their home and move to the city to join their sole remaining daughter. In spite of the adverse circumstances, Rosi enjoyed having her parents closer by, and every Friday night she and Hermann would make the long walk across town (Jews were no longer permitted to ride public transportation) to share Sabbath dinner at the Eckstein's apartment. Along the way, their route took them past one of the city's main synagogues. One week, as they walked along the street in front of the temple, Hermann and Rosi noticed that vandals had broken in and ransacked the sanctuary.

One morning not long afterward, Gestapo agents appeared at their apartment without warning. Heart pounding, Rosi went to answer the insistent rapping on the door. The two men commanded her to step aside. They were looking for Hermann, they said, to take him in — "just for questioning." Rosi knew this was nonsense. Once Hermann was in custody, the two of them might never get a chance to escape. Thinking quickly, she told the officers that her husband was sick in bed with pneumonia and could not be moved. To her surprise, the men relented. It was still only 1937, and perhaps the Gestapo agents were not yet as aggressive as they would later become. They were skeptical though, and promised to return the following week. In the meantime, however, the officers issued an unmistakable warning: If Hermann were to somehow make a miraculous "recovery" and leave the apartment before the men returned, they would shoot him on sight in the street. Rosi shut the door and tried to compose herself. Whatever lingering doubts she and Hermann might have had about the need to leave Germany had disappeared for good.

During this same time, Reinhardt Heydrich, Hitler's deputy in charge of the SS, had been planning a major attack against the Jews. It was a young Jewish man named Herschel Grynzspan who provided the spark to action. The Nazis had recently deported Grynzpan's family to a refugee camp in Poland. Intent on retribution, he had made his way undetected by train to Paris where, on November 9, 1938, Herschel Grynzspan shot and killed Ernst vom Rath, Undersecretary to the German Ambassador to France. Heydrich seized upon the provocation and quickly launched a nationwide assault.

Even before the attack began, there had been vague rumors within the Jewish Community that something big was about to happen. No one had any notion of the full extent of the Nazis' plans, but one thing was certain: whatever the regime was up to, it was not likely to be good for the Jews. Hermann and Rosi had grown increasingly desperate. On the very day of the assassination in Paris, Hermann had gone again to the American Consulate in Stuttgart to beg for their entry visas — only to return once more empty handed. With speculation rampant, the two of them knew that they had to get out of their own apartment. If something did happen, that was sure to be the first place that the Gestapo would come looking for Hermann. They talked about moving in with one or another of their parents, but that option didn't seem like it would be any safer. Both the Baers and the Ecksteins lived in the heavily Jewish eastern section of the city, which would be swarming with Gestapo agents if some major campaign against the Jews were to begin.

Short on good options, Hermann and Rosi turned to the only non-Jew they knew they could trust — Friedrich Zins. The Praunheim district where my grandparents lived contained relatively few Jewish families, and because of that Hermann and Rosi hoped that the Gestapo might not

43

come looking for them there. They were not sure if Friedel and Selma would be willing to provide them with a hiding place, and they knew they had no right to ask their sister and brother-in-law to put themselves in such grave danger. They need not have worried.

I'm sure my grandparents were well aware that if the Gestapo found them hiding Jews in their apartment, all four of them (and maybe the children too) would be arrested and probably sent away to prison camp. The family's apartment was not particularly conducive to hiding either. With only 800 square feet of living space, there was no place for two extra people to remain unseen. Friedel and Selma could have come up with plenty of excuses why they should not get involved, but in the end, they weren't about to just sacrifice Hermann to the Nazis. Ignoring the danger, my grandparents opened their doors to Selma's Jewish relatives. One day before the attack on the Jews began, Hermann and Rosi took up residence in the tiny hallway at the back of their apartment, dubbed by Friedel and Selma as their "veranda."

"The 'Veranda' as it appears today (dimensions unchanged from the 1930s)"

III. KRISTALLNACHT

The pogrom began in the early morning hours of November 10, 1938. Organized groups of Nazi sympathizers fanned out across the country, setting fire to virtually all of the 275 synagogues in Germany. Local fire trucks stood nearby by pre-arrangement — not to extinguish the blaze, but to prevent the fire from spreading to adjacent non-Jewish buildings. Roving squads of vandals broke into Jewish homes and businesses, smashing the glass on Jewish storefronts. The shattered debris lay in the streets, looking to some like fine crystal and giving name to a night that glittered with violence and devastation. Inexplicably, the marauding bands completely bypassed Hermann and Rosi's apartment. Across town however, Rosi's parents were not nearly so lucky. Looters ransacked the Eckstein's apartment, and Nazi agents arrested Rosi's father. Had Hermann chosen to seek refuge with his in-laws that night, the Gestapo would certainly have swept him up as well.

"Frankfurt's Börneplatz synagogue burning during the Kristallnacht"

By November 11, after an endless night and day of rioting, Gestapo agents had imprisoned more than one in ten Jews nationwide — over 2,600 Jewish men in Frankfurt alone. The Nazis had intended to target primarily the young and able-bodied, but inevitably in the chaos and confusion, many elderly and handicapped Jews were scooped up as well. Wilhelm Eckstein, then age fifty-four, was one of the unlucky ones. After the pogrom officially ended on November 16, authorities released a few of the older men, but for Rosi's father the nightmare had just begun.

In the first few days following the *Kristallnacht*, the Nazis dispatched two large transports from Frankfurt to concentration camps at Buchenwald, Dachau and Sachsenhausen. Over five hundred Jewish prisoners were assembled in the *Festhalle* convention center, loaded onto buses, and driven to the train station in the southernmost part of the city. Guards forced the men to hold heavy suitcases for hours and to sing Nazi songs extolling the persecution of Jews. When it was finally time to go, they beat the deportees with clubs and sticks as they herded their captives onto the train cars. Some victims fell under the blows, and many more tried to stop and pray, angering their captors even more and intensifying the physical abuse. Many hours later, the train carrying the Frankfurt Jews reached the outskirts of Munich. Fresh guards transferred Wilhelm Eckstein and the other prisoners into locked cattle cars for the final leg of their journey to Dachau, packing them so tightly that the men scarcely had room enough to breathe or turn around.

To a man, the Jews were stunned. The whole thing had happened so quickly. They were law-abiding citizens who had done nothing wrong. Many of them had even fought for their country in the Great War. How could they be treated like this? *Schutzhaft* ("protective custody") was the term the Nazis used to justify these early deportations, but this lame attempt at subterfuge fooled no one. Arriving at last at Dachau, Wilhelm Eckstein became simply Prisoner No. 30334.

Once at the camp, workers shaved the prisoners' heads, distributed cloth number patches for the men to sew onto their civilian clothing, and made each new inmate officially state his preferred method of execution — shooting or hanging. Guards also forced the Jews to turn over all of their personal possessions. The men received receipts for their valuables, but of course most of these items were never returned, even when their owners were later released. Lastly, the prisoners had to strip naked before shuffling outside into the November cold, where they were sprayed with cold water, ostensibly to "disinfect" them. Once processed and inside the gates, the Jews found themselves completely cut off from the outside world, unable to get word of their whereabouts to families or loved ones back home.

Chaos reigned in those early camps. Originally constructed for political prisoners, these facilities were not intended to accommodate such a large and sudden influx of people. In marked contrast to the later efficiency of Nazi mass extermination facilities, operations in 1938 were in near-total disarray. For two full days, the new arrivals received no food or water of any kind. Finally, on the afternoon of November 18, guards distributed a thin goulash to the starving prisoners, after which many of the men promptly fell ill with diarrhea. Prisoners were restricted to just ¼ liter of water each per day for all uses — even the guards had to make do with only twice that amount. The extreme lack of water made personal hygiene impossible. Filth was everywhere and disease rampaged among the inmates. At Dachau, lethal epidemics of typhus and meningitis spread throughout the crowded barracks.

In the six weeks immediately following the *Kristallnacht*, 227 Jewish men died in Nazi concentration camps. This number now seems small in contrast to the atrocities that came afterwards, but it marked the first time that Hitler's regime had systematically and intentionally murdered such a large group of Jews all at once. At each camp, special squads of prisoners collected and cremated the dead. Because of the general disarray, many of those who died in those first few days and weeks were never properly registered or accounted for, and their relatives simply never heard from their husbands, fathers, and sons again. Some of the luckier families did receive notification that a death had occurred — always officially from "natural causes". The message invariably came coupled with a demand to retrieve a box of ashes at some designated time and place in the prisoner's home city. For most, this was the first news of any kind that they had received since seeing their loved one being dragged away weeks before.

In December 1938, the Nazis began to release some of the men who had survived those first awful weeks. As they departed the camp in stages, the prisoners once again had their heads shaved — a reminder of the humiliation they had endured and part of the regime's psychological war against its Jewish victims. Those fortunate enough to regain their freedom were required to sign personal statements certifying that their captors had not mistreated them. Rosi's father was released on December 21 and returned to his family a day or two later. During Wilhelm Eckstein's absence, the mood among the remaining Jews in Frankfurt had changed dramatically. Even those who had refused to acknowledge the threat before could no longer deny that the situation had irreparably altered. No Jew could now hope to live openly in Germany, and outlasting the Nazis was no longer an option.

Even after things had quieted down again in Frankfurt, Hermann and Rosi remained fearful. They had stayed in Friedel and Selma's apartment for several more days after the *Kristallnacht* ended, until they were sure that the deportations had finally ended. At the time, my grandparents believed that no one outside their small family knew that they were hiding Jews, but they were mistaken. Years later, my mother talked with one of her former neighbors, a man whose father owned the beauty shop next door to my grandparent's apartment. Friedrich Boneberger told her that several of the neighbors were well aware of what her parents were doing, which is hardly surprising. Given the close quarters, it would have been impossible for the neighbors not to catch a glimpse of Hermann and Rosi from time to time, but somehow the knock on the door from the Gestapo never came.

With the immediate danger passed, Hermann and Rosi returned briefly to their own apartment, knowing they couldn't stay. The Gestapo was sure to come looking for Hermann again before long. With no better alternatives, they moved in with Hermann's parents at their apartment at Musikantenweg 39, in the old Jewish section of the city, around the corner from Berthold Baer's now-shuttered shoemaker's shop. Each day, Rosi would walk across town to the couple's old apartment, anxiously hoping to find an envelope from the US Consulate. At the end of November, the long-awaited visas at last appeared in their mailbox.

On January 1, 1939, as required by Nazi law, Hermann and Rosi officially notified the police that they were giving up their apartment and would stay with Hermann's parents while waiting to leave the country. They also had to certify that neither of them had any outstanding debts (other than to fellow Jews) and that they possessed no financial assets or other items of value remaining in Germany. Their official list of possessions now consisted of just two suitcases full of clothing and a separate small bundle of personal items.

It was a bittersweet time for all of them. Fear of what would become of the loved ones left behind tempered any relief that Hermann and Rosi felt at their imminent escape. How would they know what was happening back in Germany? Would they really all be reunited in America one day? Near the end of January, possibly overwhelmed by the stress of helping his son prepare to flee, Berthold Baer suffered a massive stroke that left him completely paralyzed on his right side.

A few short days later, with Berthold still lying immobile in his hospital bed, the time had come for Hermann and Rosi to go. Hermann was reluctant to leave with his father's condition so unstable, but he knew he had no choice. On Tuesday February 21, Hermann and Rosi left on foot for Frankfurt's main train station. Jenny, Selma, and both of Rosi's parents went with them. No one said much along the way. The Ecksteins had been through this earlier, when their other two children had left the country two years before. They fought to hold back the tears as the last of their offspring was about to make good her escape. Before long, the small party reached the foot of the platform. Hermann and Rosi said their final good-byes and boarded a passenger train bound for the port at Cherbourg, France. As the locomotive pulled out of the station, Selma tried her best to console Jenny. After the train was no longer in sight, she offered to walk her mother home, but Jenny refused. She needed some time alone to think before going back to the hospital to face her husband in his fragile state.

~:~

I never had the chance to ask my grandparents while they were still alive whether they had hesitated at all before making the decision to offer refuge to their Jewish relatives. By 1938, my grandfather certainly had enough to worry about just trying to hold onto his job and protect his own wife and daughters from the Nazis. Without Friedel's willingness to put himself at risk, however, Hermann almost certainly would have been swept up during the *Kristallnacht*. Had that happened, he would have lost his last chance to escape. It is no exaggeration to say that by rescuing him from deportation, Friedel almost certainly saved Hermann's life.

I also can't help wondering whether my grandparents realized until much later just how much danger they had put themselves in. When, not long before Hitler came to power, my grandfather had chosen to marry a Jewish girl he could not have imagined that he would someday have to use his own home to hide his wife's relatives from the police. But Friedrich Zins was not a man who could simply turn his back. In his heart and in his mind, there was never any question what he had to do.

IV. NO ESCAPE

After the *Kristallnacht*, more than 7,000 of Frankfurt's Jews fled from Germany, the vast majority of them in the first ten months following the November 1938 pogrom. In September of 1939, the outbreak of general war in Europe suddenly made it much more difficult to escape. The bolder and more fortunate continued to trickle out until two years later when, on October 23, 1941, the Nazi government officially closed the country's borders and halted all further emigration. Any Jews still left in the country — including all the rest of my grandmother's immediate family — were trapped.

For the longest time, I wasn't sure how to tell this part of my family's story. With my grandparents long gone, there wasn't anyone left to talk to about what it was like to live through those threatening times. Despite years digging up an astounding collection of firsthand accounts in archives on both sides of the Atlantic, I had uncovered no descriptions from my own family members about the period when the Nazis were closing off their last avenues of escape.

Then one day, I got an e-mail from my cousin in Frankfurt. True to form, Doris had been trying to pin down some minor detail about a woman named Minna Stein, a distant relative of my grandmother's who had achieved some notoriety counseling survivors of Frankfurt's Jewish Community after the war. Hermann Baer had been Frau Stein's nephew, and Doris wanted me to ask my Aunt Rosi, still lucid at nearly age ninety, if her husband had ever received any letters from his famous aunt. My mother and I had pushed Rosi to hunt for old letters once before to no avail, but now she admitted that she wasn't sure what she might still have. Rosi had recently moved into an assisted living facility, and her son had hurriedly packed forty years worth of belongings collected in her attic into boxes that had sat for weeks in his upstairs guest room, waiting to be sorted. When my mother called him, Steven Baer agreed to have a look. A couple of weeks later he called back, sounding almost apologetic. Steven hadn't found any letters from Minna Stein, but he had discovered a cache of some forty-odd letters his parents had received after their arrival in the US — letters written by their relatives stuck back in Germany. The letters ran from February 1939, when Hermann and Rosi had sailed to America, until the fall of 1942, when the last of the mass deportations of Jews from Frankfurt had taken place. Most of them seemed to have been signed by Hermann's mother Jenny. Might I be interested in having a look at those?

Scarcely able to contain our excitement, my mother and I flew to Steven's house in South Carolina the following week to get our first look at these priceless documents. What we discovered was a personal account, almost week-by-week, of what my great grandmother had been thinking as she sought in vain to find a way out of Hitler's Germany. To me, it was almost as if she were alive again to tell us her story face to face. As we sat there reading about every twist and turn in Jenny Baer's quest to get her loved ones to safety, it was obvious to me that my great grandmother had lost none of the fierce determination she had as a younger woman. How to tell the story became obvious. In the pages that follow, Jenny herself will tell you what it felt like as, one-by-one, every last chance she and her family had to escape the Nazis disappeared.

~:~

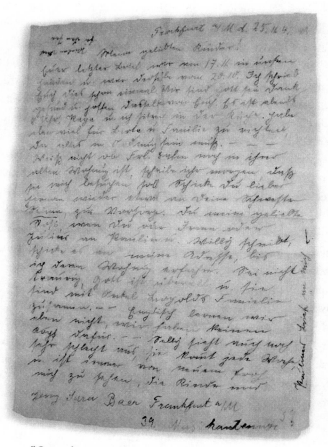

*"One of Jenny's letters – Note signature at bottom
displaying Nazi-mandated middle name of 'Sara.'"*

The story begins at the end of February 1939, two days after Jenny had launched her son and daughter-in-law off on their voyage to America. She got up very early in the morning and sat down for the first time to compose a letter to Hermann and Rosi. Selma and her daughters had been staying with Jenny to soften the blow of their loss, but still her spirits sagged. "All my hopes go with you," she wrote to her only son. A little later that day, a postcard arrived bearing the welcome news that Hermann and Rosi had arrived safely in Holland, meaning that they were at last beyond Hitler's reach. Buoyed for the moment, Jenny set out for the hospital to bring Berthold the news. Her husband, still recuperating from his stroke, had missed the send-off at the train station.

"The children should be on their way to the States by now," Jenny told Berthold when she arrived at his bedside, prompting the old man to burst into tears. After regaining control, Berthold confessed that "a great stone has been lifted from my heart." The two of them sat together, doing their best to console each other. After a while, Jenny got up, kissed her stricken husband goodbye, and made her way to her daughter Bertha's apartment, where she was expected for dinner. Jenny had been very much looking forward to this visit, and to spending some time with her grandson Karl Heinz, whom she hadn't seen for several days. That night, Karl seemed especially happy to see her too, and the few hours the two of them spent playing together helped distract Jenny from her plight for a while. Later on, Rosi's parents stopped by to chat, and afterward Jenny felt a little better about things. After dinner, the Ecksteins suggested that they walk Jenny home, an offer she eagerly accepted.

Two days later, Jenny wrote to Hermann again:

"You are really gone now, and you are crossing the ocean! When this letter reaches you, I will know that you are safe and I will be satisfied and not complain. I told your father already on Friday that you had gone. The worry about you seems to have weighed heavily on him because Saturday and today, Sunday, he was a lot better. We must fight our mixed feelings. It had to be this way dear Hermann. When you see the relatives, give them regards from me. I cannot write to everybody. I can't afford the money for the stamps. Hopefully I will get a letter from you soon. I want to hear everything. I think you will feel at home in your new country very soon. Be well and stay healthy, and think always of your loving mother."

"Jenny Baer, in happier times, May 1935"

The following day, another postcard arrived in Jenny's mailbox. Hermann and Rosi had crossed the English Channel to Southhampton, another step towards freedom. Taking the card with her, Jenny again went to the hospital to share the news. Berthold snatched it out of her hand like a small child. He sat motionless, staring at the small piece of paper he held in his one good arm. Unable to escape even from his own wheelchair, let alone follow his son to safety, the old man labored to keep his rising frustration at bay.

After arriving in England, Hermann and Rosi spent the next couple of days idling about, waiting for workers to ready their ship for the transatlantic crossing. Hermann had hoped to meet up with an old friend, Lothar Wolf, who had earlier escaped to England. Before leaving Frankfurt, Hermann had received a letter from Wolf in which his friend had talked about how thrilled he was that Hermann and his wife were about to be delivered from "Hitler's Germany and the murderers." But by the time Hermann and Rosi got to southern England, Lothar Wolf was no longer living in London. He and a group of fellow Jews had moved to a camp in Sandwich, four hours to the east by bus. British officials had promised the refugees both better living conditions and work at the relatively generous rate of ten shillings per week. Once Wolf and his companions had arrived, however, all they found was a series of dilapidated barracks outfitted with the most primitive of facilities. The perpetually cold and stormy weather near the coast further depressed the group's morale, and to make matters worse, the promised jobs had failed to materialize as well. Three thousand German Jews were now stuck sharing forty-five crude barracks, earning only a paltry eight pence each per week.

Too broke for the moment to leave, Wolf's letter had nevertheless sounded upbeat. He vowed not to remain exiled in Sandwich for long. Hermann's friend also wrote that he had recently "put everything in motion" to get his parents out of Germany too, and he felt hopeful that it would all work out somehow. By the end of the following year, Lothar Wolf did manage to find his way to America, reuniting with his parents and sister in Miami. Though they had missed each other in the confusion of their hard-won escapes, after the war Hermann and Lothar settled not far from each other in New Jersey, and they remained good friends well into old age.

With the ship's preparations finally completed, Hermann and Rosi sailed from England on February 25, 1939, bound for New York on board H.M.S. *Aquitania*. Their voyage was to be one of the last major transports of German refugees to the US before the onset of war halted the flow of escapees from Europe. The ultra-modern, "quadruple-screw" vessel had the distinction of having previously made the ocean cross-ing in the then-record time of just three days. Third-class fare for Her-mann and Rosi was set at 622 marks, a princely sum that had forced the couple to empty their bank account two months earlier to pay for their passage.

Back in Germany, Jenny had no way of knowing that her son and daughter-in-law were at last on their way. After their last postcard, sev-eral difficult days followed with no information while the two were at sea. On March 1, still waiting for news, Jenny and her husband did their best to celebrate their twenty-fifth wedding anniversary in Berthold's hospital room. Staff and fellow patients stood in for the missing family members. Though she tried to put on a brave face, Jenny found it hard to enjoy herself, weighed down as she was by so much uncertainty. Two days later, she wrote to Hermann again:

"We had a great celebration on March 1. The patients brought flowers for our silver anniversary, and the nurses did too. Word spread quickly around the hospital and everyone came to congrat-ulate us, including the doctors. There was even a blurb in the Jew-ish newsletter about it, but it was all too much for me. My mind leans not towards joyfulness, I'm too preoccupied with worry for [Bertha's husband] Jakob. From all this celebration came a conse-quence, my dear Hermann. As you always said, 'everything must be paid for.'"

I'm not sure what my great grandmother was referring to with that last statement, except perhaps to reiterate the conflicting mixture of joy and sadness they all felt over Hermann and Rosi's leaving. On March 3, 1939, the *Aquitania* steamed into New York Harbor. Two days later, word from the ship's operator reached Frankfurt that all hands had arrived safely in the US. It was time now for Selma and her daugh-ters to return to their own home, and with Berthold still stuck in the hospital, all at once Jenny felt completely alone in her empty apartment. The possibility that she might never see Hermann and Rosi again had suddenly grown much too real.

For Friedel and Selma, in contrast to their Jewish relatives, daily life had not changed all that much. As long as my grandmother remained married to her Aryan husband, Selma remained protected, and thankfully the Gestapo seemed little interested in her two mixed-breed daughters as well. Still, despite a need to emigrate that was clearly less acute, my grandparents harbored the hope that they, too, would one day have the opportunity for a fresh start in America.

Even before the eye-opening events of November 1938 had taken place, all of my grandmother's family members had applied for permission to emigrate to the US. Other than Hermann and Rosi, however, whose quota number of 5,281 had been by far the lowest, no one else in the family had come close to getting their entry visa. Jenny and Berthold were next in line at number 15,359, but they still couldn't travel because of Berthold's disability. After the Baers came Rosi's parents, at number 17,443, followed by Selma's sister Bertha and her husband, at 20,103. My grandparents, at number 38,641, were hopelessly down the list.

Painfully aware of how slowly the Americans seemed to be letting people into the country, Friedel and Selma resigned themselves to a lengthy wait. "A chess game," was how my grandfather often referred to the immigration process. They would submit all the required paperwork believing that everything was in order, only to find out weeks later that some document or other was still missing. A flurry of activity would follow, while Friedel and Selma tried to comply with the new request. This same scenario repeated itself over and over as my grandparents, along with all the others hoping to make it to the US, tried to fight their way through a bureaucracy whose main goal appeared to be to prevent them from getting in.

From time to time, my grandparents would talk with their daughters about their dreams of a new life outside Germany, but for the most part they chose not to burden the girls with things they couldn't do anything about. My mother remembers clearly that the prospect of leaving behind everything that was familiar did not frighten her as a child. She and her sister knew that once they got to America they would be rejoining many of the relatives they already knew, and besides, as long as their parents were with them, the two girls felt confident that things would always work out all right. From time to time, Erika and Inge even wrote letters to their aunt and uncle in America, speaking hopefully of a time when the whole family would be together again in their newly adopted country.

In the meantime, there were plenty of things to distract young girls from the troubled world around them. Like kids in more normal times, they loved to play outside with their friends. They also enjoyed helping their father take care of his bunnies. As food rationing became ever more restrictive, Friedel had taken to raising rabbits in the backyard to augment the family's meager protein consumption. This was great fun for Erika and Inge, even if they knew that their furry pets were ultimately fated to end up on the dinner table.

The Praunheim district where my grandparents lived contained relatively few fully Jewish families, but mixed-religious couples (*Mischehen*, in official Nazi parlance) were not uncommon. The Jewish partners in these marriages, like Selma, were largely spared from discrimination, but many others around them were not so lucky. The Gallinats, for example (parents of Erika's ally from the schoolyard incident), were frequently harassed because they were Communists — a group the Nazis despised almost as much as they hated the Jews. The man who owned the beauty shop next door to Friedel and Selma's apartment also became a target. For the crime of having had one Jewish grandmother, the Nazis slated Alex Boneberger to be one of the first deportees to their newly opened concentration camp at Mathausen. Ever resourceful however, my grandparents' neighbor scrambled to cut a deal with his Gestapo pursuers.

For the duration of the war, he agreed to provide Nazis officials with free haircuts in exchange for his continued freedom.

By early 1939, the impulse to escape among Germany's remaining Jewish population had reached panic proportions. As the number of those leaving the country increased steadily, Jews also fled inward from the countryside to the relative safety of the big cities. Jews living in the smaller villages had always had a harder time staying inconspicuous, and as a result, they had generally suffered greater persecution than their urban counterparts. A large number of these internal refugees landed in Frankfurt. Many of those who came to the city followed relatives who had moved to Frankfurt earlier and established homes there. With the government pressuring local property owners not to rent to Jewish tenants, most new arrivals either took up residence with family members or leased rooms from other Jews. Approximately 10,800 Jews migrated to Frankfurt during the Nazi years, inadvertently aiding the regime in the process. Late in 1941, when the large-scale deportations to the camps began, most of the Jews had already collected themselves within the city limits. As a result, the Gestapo found the job of rounding up their victims greatly simplified.

The majority of the internal refugees came to Frankfurt hoping it would be just a stopping off point before leaving Germany for good, but often things didn't work out that way. A critical lack of funds complicated the efforts of most Jewish families to escape the Nazi persecution. There was little work available except in domestic service to other Jews, and few could still afford such luxuries. Jewish residents who could not prove current employment often wound up conscripted into forced labor battalions instead. Hours were long and, although the Jews received some compensation for this work, wages were set well below subsistence levels. As a result, large numbers of Jewish households lapsed into poverty. For many, taking in other Jews as boarders became the only way they could make ends meet.

As rural residents gradually replaced the wealthy and educated Jews who had been disproportionately successful in escaping the country, the character of Frankfurt's Jewish population began to change. One-by-one, Jewish businesses and cultural institutions closed down and contacts among friends and business associates were lost. The Jews of Frankfurt had long prided themselves on taking care of their own, but now Jewish self-help organizations that had existed for decades or centuries were disappearing at the very moment in history that the population needed them the most. Slowly and inexorably, the Nazis dismantled whatever sense of community remained among their victims.

Throughout 1939, the regime accelerated its attack on the Jews. On January 1, a new edict required all Jews to re-register with the government and to add a new middle name—Sara for the women and Israel for the men—thus updating the Gestapo's list of potential targets in the process. On January 30, Adolf Hitler publicly announced his intention to exterminate the Jewish race in Europe. In response, local officials further tightened the already meager food rations for the Jews and in Frankfurt, city police stepped up their arrests of members of the Jewish Community.

During this time, though free of the Nazi threat, Hermann and Rosi were nevertheless struggling. Having focused so intensely on eluding Hitler's grasp, they had had little chance to think about what came afterwards. Like many new immigrants, the two of them had harbored the romantic notion that Americans would welcome them warmly, but the reality turned out to be quite different.

Having arrived virtually penniless, Hermann and Rosi had few choices about where to live. Rosi's sister Irma, already in the US for a couple of years by the time her younger sister landed, had arranged for the new arrivals to rent a room in an apartment on W. 180th Street, in the Washington Heights section of Manhattan. Another German immigrant had leased the flat, keeping one room for her own family and subletting out the rest to make the rent. Hermann and Rosi took up residence in the living room, where they slept on a sofa "alive with bedbugs," as Rosi described it to me many years later. Julius Eckstein, Rosi's younger brother, had rented one of the bedrooms in the same apartment. Thirteen people shared a five-room apartment with a single bathroom. Each morning before work, the men stood in the hallway outside the washroom door, lining up for a turn to shave. After six long and crowded months, Hermann and Rosi had saved up enough to move into a place of their own. They chose their new home carefully, trying to make sure that they would have enough left over from their combined weekly earnings of $48 to still be able to help their relatives back in Germany. Their new apartment, at 21 Broadway Terrace, cost them $36 a month.

Despite having very little English at first, Hermann had been well trained, and he quickly found work in a factory making eyeglasses. The supervisor there was a fellow Jew from Poland, who took a particularly dim view of his German counterparts. Like many others who had fled Nazi-occupied lands, Hermann's new boss believed that Jews from within the Reich were somehow to blame for Hitler's misdeeds. The German refugees, for their part, felt little fondness in return for their Eastern European brethren, whom they regarded as uneducated and lacking in cultural refinement. After his first nine months on the job, Hermann failed to receive a promised salary increase. He challenged his foreman about this, but the Polish man retorted matter-of-factly, "If I want to pay more, I don't have to hire a German Jew." Such was Hermann Baer's introduction to his new life in the Land of the Free.

Family members who had landed in other countries had it even worse. A month after Hermann set sail for America, his aunt, Selma Klein (one of Jenny Baer's sisters), left Germany with her own family, bound for Shanghai, China. The Emperor of Japan, perhaps as a way of currying favor with his erstwhile Nazi allies, was permitting Jewish refugees to enter the portion of the city he controlled. At the time, Japanese-occupied Shanghai was the only place in the entire world that Jews could flee to without needing an entry visa. But even if they could find a way to get there, European refugees faced vast hurdles in adapting to the Asian culture and language. Many families arrived without any savings, opportunities for work were scarce, and most struggled just to buy food. In her letters to Hermann, Jenny pleaded repeatedly with her son to send money to keep her sister's family from starving — not realizing perhaps that every dollar sent to China drained the very same resources needed to help get the rest of the family out of Germany. After mid-1940, no further news came from Selma Klein in Shanghai. Jenny briefly considered trying to search for her sister through the German Consulate there, but she was much too preoccupied with her own problems to pursue the matter with any vigor.

When not working, Hermann and Rosi spent much of their free time trying to help the rest of their family members emigrate. Whatever money they could spare they sent in $30 increments to Jenny and Berthold, usually wiring the funds through Selma to reduce the chance of interception by the Gestapo. In April and July of 1940, having accumulated what they hoped was enough cash, the couple submitted signed affidavits to the American Consulate in Stuttgart, pledging support for both sets of parents as well as for Hermann's half-sister Bertha and her family. With combined wages of less than $50 per week and savings of only $1,088, however, they were far short of the $10,000 in assets that US immigration law required for each new immigrant. It didn't matter. Their increasing alarm for the loved ones they had left behind forced them to apply anyway, hoping that US authorities would deem their meager incomes to be sufficient and make an exception under the circumstances. It was indeed remarkable that, between supporting themselves and sending whatever extra they could back to Germany and China, Hermann and Rosi had been able to save anything at all.

Back in Germany, trying to exert what little control she could over the deteriorating situation, Jenny concentrated her own efforts on the search to find an alternative sponsor. Despite the fact that Berthold remained completely paralyzed after months of therapy, the two of them continued to talk, in Jenny's words, "day and night" about their strategy for getting out. In the year since he had left the hospital, Berthold had rarely been out of the couple's apartment. Nevertheless, he and Jenny kept planning for a time when the two of them would be able to travel again. To pass the time during his long hours of immobility, Berthold taught himself English, aided by the birthday gift of a new eyepiece from his wife. Such necessities had become almost impossible to obtain, but Jenny had somehow finagled one out of an optometrist in their building. The old man took great pride in showing off his newfound skills, writing short letters to Hermann in English and conversing with Selma (who had taken classes at school as a youngster) in the language of their hoped-for new home.

With Selma free of immediate danger, Jenny concentrated her efforts on finding a way to get Bertha's family out first. She wrote to Manfred Linick, a good friend from her youth who had moved to the States many years before. Linick was living in Detroit, where he had built a successful vending machine company. In her letter, Jenny decided to level with her old friend. She told Linick about her own inability to leave because of her husband's poor health, and pleaded with him to sponsor her daughter's family instead, perhaps even to guarantee Bertha's husband, Jakob, a job when he got to the States. For weeks, there was no reply. The waiting was unbearable. "Everything depends on him [Linick]," Jenny wrote to Hermann. Finally, Linick's answer arrived. Jenny's old friend wrote back warmly, in a tone that suggested shared intimacy from long ago. He was sympathetic to her request, but cautious nonetheless. The US economy was sputtering, mechanization had replaced much of his need for new workers, and Linick himself had already supported the immigration of nearly thirty other friends and relatives, many of whom he still employed in his business. He was willing to provide Jakob with a job, but he could not commit to being the primary sponsor for the entire family, suggesting that this was more properly Hermann's responsibility. Jenny was distraught. Clearly, she thought, Linick did not understand the precariousness of her family's situation. With few other options, she wrote back again, pressing her friend to reconsider.

In reconstructing these events, one thing has always puzzled me. Several of Jenny's brothers had already made it to the States by this time, yet Jenny's long-standing estrangement from her family continued to get in the way of her asking them for help. The need for reconciliation could not have been more urgent, yet the reasons for Jenny's estrangement have remained obscure.

Certainly Jenny's long ago decision to marry against her parents' wishes cannot be the only explanation for the ongoing rift. One possibility is that her brothers ostracized her for what they viewed as her lack of sufficient religious devotion. Though she was quite comfortable with Jewish ritual in general, Jenny's level of observance contrasted sharply with that of her far more devout brothers. Intensifying these divisions, both of Jenny's daughters had married outside the faith, violating a long-standing Jewish taboo against mixed marriages. Most Orthodox Jews take a very dim view of this practice even today. Still, given the life-and-death issues at hand, it seems incredible to me that Jenny's brothers could have turned their backs on her simply because of their religious differences. Given all that had gone before, perhaps Jenny was just too embarrassed to swallow her pride and go to her brothers for help.

My mother tried once to discuss the issue of Jenny's reluctance with her cousin, Jonah Löwenthal, the grandson of Jenny's brother Abraham. Jonah insists that he can't recall his parents or grandparents ever bringing up this sensitive subject while he was growing up. To be fair, Jonah was just a small child when these dramatic events took place. I can't help thinking, though, that there is something that has intentionally been left unsaid — if not by Jonah then by his parents, who are long since gone. Whatever the reasons, now lost to time and the family's closed ranks, Jenny never turned to her brothers in America for assistance, and they never offered any.

Another of Jenny's brothers, Leopold, was still stuck in Germany with her. Like Jenny, Leopold's most pressing concern was to find a US sponsor for one of his children. His son, Jakob, had just completed vocational training as a mechanic. Though apprehensive about the thought of leaving his family behind, the energetic eighteen-year-old was also eager for a fresh start, free of the Nazi yoke. Leopold asked Jenny which she thought would be better — to approach their brothers directly on Jakob's behalf, or to let the boy make his own appeal. In the end, he decided to take the initiative himself.

Among the Löwenthal brothers in the US, it was Abraham who had worked the hardest to maintain contact with his siblings back in Germany, even going so far on one occasion as to send Jenny some snapshots of his family in their new home. Rather than go directly to his brother for help, however, Leopold instead directed his request to Abraham's son Julius, a contemporary of his own son. Leopold also considered writing to another nephew, Kurt, but ultimately thought better of the idea. Both Jenny and Leopold regarded Kurt as more sympathetic towards them than anyone else in the family, but Hermann had already approached him a short time earlier to ask for money for Selma Klein's family in Shanghai. The two of them thought it best not to go to the same well too often.

Jenny documented this entire process in her regular correspondence with Hermann. Partly, I think, this was a form of therapy for her. Hermann had been his mother's closest confidant before he left for America, and Jenny missed having him around as she sought to lessen the growing uneasiness she felt. As she clung to the fading hope that they all would still make it out somehow, Jenny continually pressured her son to explore every possible avenue of assistance. Once, with uncharacteristic self-interest, Jenny went so far as to caution Hermann not to let the pleas of more distant friends or relatives distract him. He had much more important things to worry about, she told her son.

Selma also wrote to Hermann during this period, but the tone of her letters was decidedly different. She told her brother about how Jenny and Karl Heinz had been over to help pick some plums in the backyard, about how she was letting her hair grow out in the hopes that it would hold a perm better, and about how Erika seemed especially interested in the way the women dressed in America. She expressed her hope that "the stork" would come to her brother and sister-in-law soon — apparently a reference to the fact that Hermann and Rosi had put off starting their family until they were safely out of Germany. Selma went on to say that with her children now a little older and more self-sufficient, she and Friedel were finally able to get out more often. They especially enjoyed going to the movies together, and they had even gotten away for a long weekend alone while Erika and Inge stayed with their grandparents. Selma was also happy to report that Friedel had recently gotten a new job as a lathe operator, which meant that there was a little more money coming in to the household now. It was obvious that she was not threatened the way the rest of her relatives were.

Though they put themselves at some risk by doing so, my grandparents continued to visit with their Jewish relatives regularly. They had never been as close to that side of the family, but Selma grew more and more worried about what was happening to her mother and sister. Sundays had always been reserved for visits from Berthold and Jenny, but because of Berthold's handicap, the process of moving him across town had now become a major undertaking. Determined to find a way, Friedel devised a special chair-like contraption to allow him to carry his stricken father-in-law. He would start out in the morning by taking the #2 trolley all the way to the other end of the line to the Baer's apartment. Once there, he strapped Berthold into the seat and hoisted the unwieldy burden on his back. Friedel then edged his way down the stairs and out onto the sidewalk, before climbing the steps of the streetcar for the ride back across the city. Although there was a stop almost right in front of my grandparent's front door, the two men would stay on for a couple more blocks until they reached the end of the line, which gave my grandfather more time to maneuver the old man off the trolley car. Once safely on firm ground again, Friedel would trek back to the apartment, carrying his helpless charge all the way.

On June 9, 1940, a host of family and friends gathered at Jenny and Berthold's home to celebrate Berthold's fifty-ninth birthday. My grandparents and their daughters were all there, along with Bertha and her whole family, including newest son Artur. "Addi," as everyone called him, had developed into an energetic toddler whose effervescent antics helped brush back, however briefly, the ever-worsening sense of dread that encircled the adults. The Ecksteins also came by that day, bringing with them a homemade cake that Rosi's mother had baked — an almost forgotten luxury with wartime rationing having bitten ever deeper into everyday life. Jenny gave her husband a new fountain pen for his birthday. It was a little thing, but it meant a lot to Berthold. He decided to reserve it specially for writing his letters to America.

Later that evening, Berthold cleared his mind and began to write to his son. More than a year had already passed since Hermann and Rosi had left for America, but the old man still felt their absence keenly. He was stung by the fact that no birthday greetings had arrived from America, and he chided his son for being so forgetful. Nevertheless, Berthold tried his best to sound upbeat. "It was a very nice day," he wrote. "Things are going well for me. The only thing I have to feel sorry about is my lameness, but I hope that I will become healthy again."

By early July, Jenny's tolerance for all the waiting was on the wane. She prompted Hermann once again for guidance:

"Dear Hermann, at the moment I don't know what I should do about Linick. Up till now, I have received no news from him. Maybe it's just too soon. Surely he will give us the sponsorship. I feel completely unsettled. If he sends the documents, it would be better if he sends them directly to me rather than to [the Consulate in] Stuttgart. Without the affidavit in hand I can do nothing. He must not understand how urgent this is. Maybe I should inquire of him one more time? Or will that make everything fall apart? It's terrible when you have no one to go to for advice. You are great, but so far away. By the time your answer can come, the time for decision is already past."

Three weeks later, she wrote again. As distraught as she was, Jenny still could not bring herself to ask her brothers for help:

"If you only knew how heavily the worries weigh one down. Still we have no news from Linick. The need for the affidavit has become even more urgent now that Jakob has received a letter from England. We sent photographs, his birth certificate and a doctor's statement. All that is missing is the pledge of support. I have written two more letters to Linick, but they could not have gotten there yet—one was sent eight days ago and one two days ago. Listen to me Hermann—please write to Linick again yourself. Tell him that after the letter from London, everything depends on him. He should at least make himself heard. It's now come to the point that if he refuses, I will go to the relatives. I have reason to think that it would be better if you write one more time. I'm so restless. He should answer you—your letter won't get lost in the mail."

After the outbreak of war in late 1939, the number of Jews leaving Germany dwindled to a lucky few. Inside the country, the Nazi government was busy imposing ever-harsher restrictions on its victims. Mail service between America and the Continent became increasingly unreliable, and eventually Jenny's regular correspondence ceased. For many long months, Hermann and Rosi had no way of knowing what was happening to the loved ones they had left behind.

A new curfew prohibited Jews from leaving their homes between the hours of 8 PM and 6 AM each day. After September 12, 1939, the regime restricted Jews to shopping only in specially designated stores, and then only during very limited hours. These authorized Jewish outlets were usually poorly stocked, and often Jews would wait in line for hours without ever knowing if there were any goods left to purchase. Finding food, coal for heating, and the other essentials of life became an all-consuming challenge. A few good-hearted Germans continued to try to help their Jewish neighbors, giving them any extra food they had or allowing them to shop illegally in the stores they owned, though anyone who associated with Jews put himself at risk of being hauled in for questioning by the Gestapo. On September 23, 1939, the Nazi government made it illegal for any Jew to own a radio, a crime now punishable by deportation or death. With the Party also in control of the newspapers, it quickly became impossible for Jews to get reliable news about the events affecting their lives. In their hunger to find out what was going on, many Jewish families defied the ban, keeping their contraband radios carefully hidden and taking them out only at night to listen to the BBC, one of the few remaining sources of uncensored information coming into the country.

In late April 1940, mail service resumed temporarily. At last, Jenny was able to communicate with Hermann in America again, but nothing much had changed. Despite her repeated pleadings, Manfred Linick had still not sent the affidavits she had asked him for, and Jenny had failed to find any other source of support. Berthold's condition was also unimproved. His disability kept him confined to his wheelchair twenty-four hours a day, and there was little hope of the two of them ever being able to travel.

On June 4, 1940, a breakthrough of sorts occurred. The US Consulate in Stuttgart notified Rosi that her parents would be eligible to receive their entry visas during the upcoming immigration year beginning in July. In the same letter, however, consular officials went on to inform her that her income, even when combined with that of her brother and sister, would be insufficient to support the new immigrants. All refugees entering the United States at the time were subject to the so-called "Public Charge Rule," which mandated strict financial requirements in order to insure that new arrivals would not become a burden on taxpayers. Given the imminent dangers facing German Jews, this policy strikes one nowadays as unnecessarily harsh. In the context of the times, however, with the US still not completely recovered from the worst depression in its history, immigration officials were under direct orders not to swamp the country's shores with penniless refugees from a distant war.

Even if they could somehow find a way to satisfy US immigration requirements, the Ecksteins would still have to find a way to pay for the journey itself. Hermann and Rosi had saved up an extra $700, enough to hold a space for them on a private passenger ship operated by the Hamburg-American Line. The ship's operators were adamant however: they would not permit Rosi's parents to board one of the company's vessels until the US Consulate notified them that a new affidavit of support from someone with "stronger financial standing" had arrived. More weeks and months passed, as family members on both sides of the Atlantic frantically sought to find a solution to the sponsorship problem. Hermann and Rosi appealed to anyone they could think of to help. Hermann wrote to Jakob Bamberger, a distant relative of Jenny's, whose family later founded the New York area department store chain of the same name, but initially there was no response. They also went back to Morris Baer, who had been their own sponsor scarcely eighteen months before, but Hermann's uncle was reluctant to make such a big commitment again. The two of them were certain that Uncle Morris had enough savings, but they also knew that as a retiree, he had no ongoing source of income. The more they pushed to find an answer, the more the sad truth became clear: most of those who had successfully fled to the US, like Morris Baer and Manfred Linick, were simply over-committed, having already helped to rescue as many friends and relatives from Germany as they could. Even as they sensed that time was running out, Uncle Morris and the others continued to hesitate.

In the end, Hermann and Rosi ran out of people to ask.

While the search for a sponsor went on, other members of my grandmother's family inched their way up the visa list. Bertha Marx sat only 3,000 names behind the Ecksteins. As her number got closer to the top, Selma's sister felt spurred to write to Hermann and Rosi herself, trying to remain hopeful:

> "Above all I want to write my thanks for what you are doing for us. I can't express it in words, but you know me well dear Hermann and you know what is in my mind. Jakob also wants to express his thanks for your sponsorship of us. He can't write himself because he is always working. Dear Rosi, I wish that I were already with you. I know you would have so much joy with our Addi."

Karl Heinz, Bertha's ten-year-old son, also added a few words of his own to his Uncle Hermann:

> "I will be very happy when we can walk through New York City together, and you can show me all the sights."

Unlike most other Jews, Bertha's family at least had some money coming in. Jakob, her husband, wasn't earning much as a forced laborer, but he was the only member of the family who still had any income at all. Still, it wasn't easy. Since the Nazis had barred Jews from using public transportation, Jakob had to leave the house before six o'clock each morning to make the long walk to the factory, rarely returning until well after six in the evening. Realizing that they had to lighten the burden on the family's only breadwinner, Bertha and Jakob decided to move closer to his place of work. On May 15, 1940, they moved into a new apartment at Kleine Wollgraben 8. The rent there, at only twenty-five marks per month, was just over half of what they had been paying before, and their new home also happened to have a very nice terrace.

They were now much further away from the rest of the family, however, which Jenny for one found rather ironic. She mused about what a joy it would have been for Berthold to come to visit and sit outside — if only they could have found a way to get him there.

As spring slipped into summer and her sixtieth birthday approached, Jenny burned with anxiety. She tried to keep herself busy by visiting friends and caring for her grandchildren, but she couldn't stop worrying about what was going to happen to all of them. Jenny had grown especially fond of Addi, and thankfully, her newest grandson was much too young to notice the troubling events going on around him. The little boy radiated life, constantly in motion and almost never in a bad mood. Even on her darkest days, Jenny could count on little Addi to brighten her spirits. Jenny must have spoken with him frequently about her son and daughter-in-law in America, because the two-year-old, who could not possibly have remembered them, nevertheless made a habit of kissing Hermann and Rosi's picture whenever he came to his grandmother's apartment to visit. For Jenny, the time she spent with her grandchildren was the only real respite she could find as she watched her family's options for escape vanish one by one.

On Saturday, June 9, 1940, the family gathered once again at the Baer's apartment on Musikantenweg, this time to celebrate Jenny's birthday. Bertha and her family, brother Leopold, Friedel and Selma and their girls, and a host of other friends and relatives were all present, but just like her husband, what Jenny really longed for was the chance to see Hermann and Rosi again. That night, when she sat down to write to him, Jenny spoke to her son of being "no longer young anymore," hinting for the first time that the possibility of their being reunited was forever slipping away.

Later that same month, Bertha and Jakob's quota number finally came up, but still they lacked a sponsor. US authorities gave the couple an additional two months to obtain the required affidavits of support before their opportunity to leave Germany would pass to the next family in line. As Bertha and Jakob agonized over the impossibility of finding a sponsor for the entire family, they reluctantly came to the decision they had been trying to avoid all along. Their only chance would be to split up. Perhaps the separation might only be temporary, or at least so they hoped. Maybe with the addition of Jakob's income once he was in the States, consular officials would relent and grant entry visas for the rest of the family. Bertha wrote to Hermann and Rosi to ask them modify their earlier affidavits, specifying support of Jakob alone. This they did willingly, but it was still not enough to satisfy US officials.

Frantic, Jenny now placed the entire burden squarely with Hermann:

"I know it is a great deal that I have laid on your young shoulders, but perhaps you can still help Jakob. You can imagine how difficult it must have been for him to have to decide to leave without his family. Has Linick still not given an answer? Should we write again, or should we try to get additional support elsewhere? All our hopes rest with you my dear child."

Hermann decided to appeal to Manfred Linick one last time. His attempts to recruit other friends or relatives to help had all proven fruitless. Once again, Hermann pushed Linick to make a commitment, this time to sponsor just Jakob alone. As the summer wore on, Jenny continued her weekly letters to Hermann, her tone becoming ever more demanding as the frustration of waiting helplessly in Germany for any kind of positive news dragged her down. Finally, on August 20, Linick gave in. Suddenly, at about the same time, Jakob Bamberger agreed to help as well. Both men executed the necessary documents on August 24, but it was too late. The affidavits could not reach Germany in time, and Bertha and Jakob's last chance to escape was gone.

Several more weeks passed. On November 5, 1940, Jenny wrote to Hermann one more time. Her frustration had peaked, but still she refused to give up all hope. If they could just present the documents to the Consulate, she told her son, perhaps it would still be possible to overcome the bureaucratic obstacles in their paths. Then, just for a moment, she let her guard down:

"I'm being very level headed, but I would give anything if I could see you again dear Hermann. You have changed so much. If I wasn't so reasonable and I really let my mind call out for help, then I would ask you for sponsorship for *myself*. But I have no *Angst*. I'll be rational and never leave my place by Papa's side. I will never *willingly* be parted from my sick husband, the one who cannot walk. I'll be like the captain who goes down with his ship. So while it *cannot* be for us, we must see that Bertha and her family are successful. Please Hermann, put *all* your energy into helping them at least.... Every hour is costly.... I don't need to tell you how urgent everything is.... If it is possible I will write about my concerns to the relatives. It is their human obligation to help their direct relatives, and Bertha is one of them."

At last, the conflicting emotions that Jenny had carried with her for so many months had boiled to the surface. On November 18, she wrote again. Her defenses were back in place, though still a little shaky:

"It's been 3 weeks already with no letter from you. I know Hermann that you have very little time. I'm sure that mail will come tomorrow. At the moment I'm just waiting impatiently for your letter, as I am hoping to hear good news soon from the relatives. Here people have become a little charged up lately and conditions are not as onerous. There is talk that things may ease up a little. Have you heard anything about this over there? Our health status is about the same; we're just becoming more and more anxious. It would help us to hear from you often, even if it's just something short.... My dear children, give all your effort for Jakob. For sure one more sponsor will be enough. People that were first notified that their documents were insufficient are now being notified that their papers are sufficient .... I wait in suspense for your letter. Bertha asks me repeatedly whether you have written yet. Friedel asks too if there is still no news from Hermann. A holy duty rests on your shoulders, may God allow you to succeed."

The weeks rolled by and progress stalled. Like Bertha and Jakob Marx, Rosi's parents also remained in limbo, waiting in vain for a sponsor to appear. Hermann tried his luck once more with Jakob Bamberger, but this time Bamberger said that he could do no more. Then, in mid-1941, responding to the spreading war in Europe, the American government abruptly changed its immigration policy. Jewish refugees could now no longer travel directly from Germany to the US. The number of Jews able to leave the Reich, already sharply reduced, dwindled almost to zero.

The only chance left for the Ecksteins would be to get out through a neutral third country. This time, the plan was for Rosi's parents to travel by train to Lisbon, where they would board a Portuguese-flagged vessel bound for New York. Money was once again an issue. Without additional cash in hand, confirming another spot on an actual ship would be impossible. Hermann and Rosi tried to get their deposit back from the Hamburg-American Line, but the refund was slow in appearing. It took several more weeks of scrimping and saving for Hermann and Rosi to put together another $700. Then, with the help of the Joint Distribution Committee, a Jewish philanthropic organization based in New York City, they were able to secure a new booking for the Ecksteins. The sponsorship issue, however, was still blocking the way. Eventually, after several more weeks spent wending their way through the interminable bureaucracy at the Hamburg-American Lines, Hermann and Rosi did get their original deposit back, but it was nowhere near enough to make a difference this late in the game.

At the end of September 1941, the Nazi government halted all further emigration from Germany to the US. By that time, over 14,000 of Frankfurt's Jews had successfully fled the country. For ten thousand others, however, including my grandmother Selma Zins, her parents Jenny and Berthold Baer, her sister Bertha Marx with husband Jakob and their two boys, and Rosi's parents Wilhelm and Pauline Eckstein, time had simply run out.

One last glimmer of hope remained. Hermann and Rosi had heard rumors about a few Jews who had gotten their relatives out through Cuba. How true this was, no one really knew, but it was at least worth a try. Even in those days, the government in Cuba was legendary for its corruption, but financial requirements for that small country were also much less stringent. Cuba required only a $2000 bond in order to enter, which in theory was refundable should the refugee later leave the country. Lawyer's fees, bank charges, and transportation costs added another $550 per person, but even with those additional costs, the total was still much less than the US was demanding. Hermann located a German-Jewish refugee named Milton Adler in nearby Newark. Herr Adler had had considerable experience helping German émigrés escape via Cuba, but he was unable to offer much cause for optimism. In October 1941, Milton Adler wrote to Hermann to say that after having personally assisted hundreds of refugees, he had finally stopped trying because he "realized how futile it is to try to bring people out of Germany and the occupied territories under present conditions." Money he had previously placed on deposit for others trying to get to Cuba had simply disappeared without a trace. "Regulations of these small countries change daily and there are no methods of transportation available for months. I feel, therefore, that any money that you would spend or that I would give to you would be of absolutely no value at the present time." Adler's harsh words abruptly extinguished the last flicker of hope Hermann and Rosi had of rescuing their loved ones from the Nazis' grip.

On November 17, Hermann received another letter from his mother. Jenny's handwriting had deteriorated noticeably and her tone was now bitter and upset:

"For me to come to you in America will only succeed if the money for the Cuban visa is there but God has willed otherwise. It is too late."

Jenny went on to describe how the Gestapo had begun deporting large groups of Jews from Frankfurt. The very thing that they had all feared for so long had now come to pass. Even her own brother had just received his notice to report, though she noted that Leopold seemed to be strangely at peace with things. "One must have a lot of respect for Leopold," Jenny wrote, "His belief never waivers." Perhaps she wished now that her own faith had been stronger too. "I feel pulled to pieces," Jenny wrote to Hermann. Bertha, too, was "deeply saddened," Jenny said. The children, mercifully, still seemed unaffected.

Jenny urged her son to save his money now. "Maybe then you can help someone else. Money rules the world," she wrote. The impending deportation of her brother and his family had shaken Jenny to the core, and fatalism seemed to have replaced all hope. "I don't know how much time I'll have to write now," she said in closing. Berthold then added a few lines of his own. His condition was unchanged, and he had resigned himself to going into a nursing home. At the moment, though, there were no spaces available. "I'm not sure if Mama would come with me," he continued, obviously disturbed by the thought that the two of them might finally have to separate.

A few days later, Jenny learned that the Gestapo planned to deport Rosi's parents as well. The Ecksteins would be leaving the city on the same train as Leopold and his family. To top it all off, Selma's health problems were acting up again. Jenny wrote to her son and daughter-in-law for what turned out to be the last time:

"Rosi, when you or Irma or Julius write to your parents, send it to my address until I find out about where they'll be living. Don't be sad. God watches over everything, and they will be together with Uncle Leopold's family. We've stopped learning English; we have no head for it at the moment. Selly [Selma] hasn't been looking too good lately. She comes by every week and seems happy to see me. Friedel and the children are doing everything they can to help her. Bertha is deeply sad. She fears for the future and wants very much to be with you, but God will not permit it. Addi and Karl are well. Jakob is still working.... I'll close for now. Everyone sends their greetings. I send you my kisses with love."

Near the end of November, a letter addressed to the Eckstein children arrived in Hermann and Rosi's mailbox. It was from their father. In it, Wilhelm Eckstein wrote at length of his love for the three of them and his firm belief that, if just given the chance, he could still work productively in a new country. He spoke again of his fervent hope that they would all soon be together again in the US. Rosi's father went on to say that he and his wife were being forced to leave their apartment in the coming week, but that he would write again with their new address as soon as possible.

It was not to be. Wilhelm Eckstein had written to his children just before he and Pauline received their deportation notices. Rosi's parents hadn't realized that their forced relocation a week before was only a prelude to their being taken from the city for good. A week after sending that final letter to America, Wilhelm and Pauline Eckstein, along with Leopold Löwenthal and his entire family, and over a thousand other Jews boarded a Nazi transport bound for Riga, Latvia. None of them was ever heard from again.

V. DEPORTATION

By the early 1940s, with countries around the world imposing increasingly strict quotas on refugees from Germany, the Nazi elite realized that they could not achieve their cherished vision of racial purity through forced emigration alone. Hitler's men needed a new strategy. Frustrated at not being able to make the Reich *Judenrein* (literally "clean of Jews"), the regime's leaders formulated a new plan: the complete physical destruction of the Jewish people.

In Frankfurt, on October 17, 1941, Gestapo officers commanded Leopold Neuhaus, leader of the city's Jewish Community (*Jüdische Gemeinde*), to appear before them and surrender his membership lists. From that moment on, Rabbi Neuhaus and his organization became the Nazi's unwilling partners, forced to assist the Gestapo in preparing and notifying the 11,000 Jews living in the city of their upcoming deportations. Two days later, at 6 AM on a Sunday morning, the first large-scale roundup began. With the help of nearly a thousand German civilians and Nazi party volunteers, armed guards rushed into Jewish homes and rousted the sleeping victims from their beds. Gestapo officers idled impatiently while the stunned and disoriented Jews stuffed whatever they could carry into suitcases, before urging their new captives out into the streets at gunpoint.

The Jews were marched in large groups to the *Grossmarkthalle*, a complex of warehouses located immediately adjacent to the heavily Jewish neighborhoods in the east end of the city. The Nazis had previously commandeered the site specifically for collecting and processing

Jews slated for deportation. A railroad spur running in front of the main building provided easy access to trains originating at Frankfurt's *Ostbahnhof.* Guards herded the first group of 1,100 deportees down a flight of stairs and into a large basement room, where they forced the prisoners to remain standing for hours, still holding their heavy suitcases in their hands. Later, officers counted off the prisoners in groups of fifty and prodded them back outside, up a wide ramp, and around to the west side of the building. There, the Jews entered a series of checkpoints. At the first desk, agents compared the prisoners' names against a master registration list. Next, hired workers rifled through the victims' luggage searching for items of value. Not satisfied with the mere plundering of personal possessions, the Nazis also required the Jews to declare the location of any financial assets they were leaving behind. At the last station, deportees had to surrender their house keys and ration cards, after which their ID cards were stamped *"EVAKUIERT."* With that act, nothing more remained of the lives they had known before. This night long, step-by-step process stripped away the very identity of the Jewish prisoners. When they were done, Nazi guards at last permitted their captives to lie down and rest.

"Exterior of Grossmarkthalle 1935"

82

V. DEPORTATION

When morning came, fresh guards marched the fatigued masses to the railroad siding in front of the building and locked them inside the line of third-class passenger cars waiting there. The prisoners received no food or water during the entire two-day journey to the Jewish ghetto in the occupied Polish city of Lødz. Conditions there were no better. Between the near-starvation rations and exposure to the extreme cold of the Polish winter, almost two hundred of the Frankfurt Jews died during that first winter. The victims' bodies lay buried to this day in the local cemetery. During the following spring and fall, another 550 prisoners from that first transport were taken to Chelmno to be gassed. A fortunate few were left behind, until the Germans closed down the Lødz ghetto in the summer of 1944 and sent those who remained to Auschwitz. By the time of liberation in 1945, only three of those first 1,100 Jews deported from Frankfurt had survived.

Back in Frankfurt, plans for a second deportation were already underway. On November 11, 1941, more than a thousand more Jews were taken from the city, this time including many families with children. Unlike the first contingent, this new group was given three days' notice to prepare, but they, too, were never told of their final destination. For this second round up, regular police and SS members replaced the earlier volunteers, whose training had proved to be grossly inadequate. Jews on this latest transport faced a much longer trip—enduring six full days locked inside rail cars on their way to the western Russian city of Minsk. There, German army regulars had constructed a two-square kilometer ghetto on the outskirts of the town. Small wooden houses and two-story stone buildings arrayed on some forty streets were originally intended to house up to 85,000 indigenous White Russian Jews. Instead, while the Frankfurt contingent was en route, Nazi soldiers executed over 6,600 residents of the Minsk ghetto to make space for the newcomers. The Jews from Frankfurt arrived to find the victims' bodies, many of them infants and children, still lying in the dwellings where they had been shot.

Three or four new families crowded into each two- or three-room structure. There was no running water, food was scarce, and temperatures reached 40 degrees below zero that first winter. More than a hundred of the Frankfurt Jews died because of the harsh conditions. As in Lødz, the SS conscripted those who were well enough to work into forced labor details, which they hired out to local businesses to generate profits for the Nazi war machine. Periodically, guards carried out *"Aktionen,"* arresting small numbers of Jews who were immediately taken outside the walls and shot. When the numbers of those no longer able to work or too ill to care for themselves grew too large, officials brought in a mobile gas chamber to put such undesirables to death. By the end of the war, only nine of the more than one thousand Jews deported from Frankfurt to Minsk were still alive.

On November 22, 1941 a third transport packed with Jews left Frankfurt bound for the East. Included in this latest group were both Rosi's parents and Jenny's brother Leopold, his wife Rosalie, and their two boys Joseph and Jakob. Of the eight Löwenthal brothers and sisters, only Jenny and Leopold had failed to escape from Germany before the mass deportations began. It was a lack of money and an invalid husband that had doomed Jenny, but Leopold had freely chosen to stay. His daughter, Sitta, had earlier fled to Czechoslovakia. For a time, Leopold had hoped to take the rest of the family there and reunite with his eldest child. After the Nazis overran that country in March 1939, however, escape to the east had become impossible. Sitta Löwenthal never returned to Frankfurt after the war, and there is no evidence that she survived.

Deportees on the November 22 transport were slated to be sent to Riga, Latvia, even though Nazi higher-ups knew that the Jewish ghetto there was already seriously overcrowded. Complicating the situation further, local officials in Riga were never notified to make provisions for the influx of several thousand more inmates. With the train from Frankfurt already en route, orders came from Heinrich Himmler, Hitler's lieutenant in charge of the Gestapo, to divert the Jews to Kaunus, in Lithuania. The Frankfurt contingent arrived at their new destination a few days after similar groups from Munich and Berlin. From the railway station, guards marched the deportees more than six kilometers through the streets of Kaunus and around the existing Jewish ghetto to Fort IX, in the southeastern section of the city. Originally built in the 1800s to protect the city from Prussian invaders, the installation had been converted to a prison after WWI. Fort IX consisted of a large complex of barracks and detention cells, all surrounded by a six-meter-high wall. The Jews of Frankfurt spent a restless night locked in their cells, separated from the groups from the other cities. Behind the walls, unbeknownst to the prisoners, mass graves had already been dug.

On the morning of November 25, soldiers from the infamous *Einsatzkommando 3* assembled the deportees from Frankfurt on the parade grounds and led them through a series of morning calisthenics designed to allay their suspicions. Next, guards herded the Jews outside the walls of the Fort, where they forced their victims at gunpoint to lie down in the open graves. Prisoners who collapsed or attempted to flee were shot in their tracks. Next, on the order of *Kommandant* Karl Jäger, machine gunners hidden on the walls high above opened fire on the helpless Jews. Most were killed instantly, but some were only wounded, and a few were not injured at all. In the end, it made no difference. Nazi soldiers bulldozed the living right along with the dead. No one, not a single person from any of the three transports, survived the massacre. The *Einsatzkommando*, widely regarded as the most prolific killers on the eastern front, murdered 2,934 Jews that day, including at least 175 children. Four days later, Jews from Vienna and Brünn met a similar fate.

Considerable historical debate has surrounded the question of why the Jews who were destined for Riga were immediately put to death at Kaunas instead, but the reason seems glaringly obvious. In late 1941, Hitler's men were completely unprepared for the practical consequences of translocating large numbers of Jewish deportees. Nazi ideology — the desire to cleanse the Reich of its Jewish inhabitants — had clearly gotten ahead of operational planning. The killings in Kaunus marked the first step in the implementation of the regime's newly adopted Final Solution, yet the executions there were less a result of prior intent than a desperate contingency measure to deal with the overcrowding at Riga. Though they might not have survived the war in any case, both the Ecksteins and Leopold Löwenthal's family paid for the Nazis' lack of preparation with their lives. On November 30, 1941, a few days after the events at Kaunus, *Reichsführer* Himmler ordered a halt to the shootings of Jews transported from within the Reich. A six-month moratorium on deportations followed, while the government paused to reconsider its strategy.

Across the ocean in America, Rosi and her sister and brother had no way of knowing that the Nazis had brutally murdered their parents. In his last, loving letter to his children, Wilhelm Eckstein had promised to write again soon with his new address, but of course no such letter ever arrived. In the week following the Ecksteins' deportation, the only news that came from Germany was a letter from Jenny to Hermann and Rosi — the last complete letter that the two of them would ever receive from the family members they had left behind. In her note, Jenny relayed personal greetings from Wilhelm and Pauline to their children — feelings the couple must have expressed just before the Gestapo took them away. "Don't be sad," Jenny wrote, "God watches over all, and your parents are with Leopold's family."

In December 1941, the United States entered the war in Europe. Regular mail service between the US and Germany ceased, putting an end to Jenny's correspondence with her son in New York for good. After that, communication between the two of them was limited to infrequent short notes, three or four lines at a time, transmitted with heavy censorship through the International Red Cross. Messages often arrived many weeks after they had been written. Instead of the long, detailed, emotional letters that she had sent before, Jenny could now send only the briefest expressions of her love, along with the news that at least those remaining in Frankfurt were still alive. News reports about Nazi atrocities were becoming more and more commonplace in the West, but all Hermann and Rosi could do was to hope for the best. The last Red Cross message from Jenny arrived in New York on August 20, 1942. She had written it fully two months before. After that, Hermann and Rosi had no way of knowing what was happening to their loved ones back in Germany.

Throughout the early months of 1942, the Nazis resumed implementing their blueprint for exterminating the Jews. In occupied Czechoslovakia, German soldiers evacuated the entire civilian population of Terezin, transforming the once-sleepy village into the concentration camp known as Theresienstadt. By the middle of the year, everything was finally in place for Hitler's men to restart the program of mass deportations to the camps.

On September 13, the Gestapo assembled another large group of Frankfurt's Jews for deportation, this time including Jenny and Berthold Baer, as well as their son-in-law Jakob Marx. Two days later, having assured themselves that they had accounted for everyone on their list, Gestapo agents took the prisoners by truck to the main train station downtown. Several hours later, a locomotive lumbered in on Track 40, trailing a long line of passenger cars behind it. Almost fourteen hundred Jews crammed aboard for the trip east, arriving the following day in Theresienstadt. Berthold Baer, still debilitated and wheelchair-bound, survived only seventeen days. Despite her grief, Jenny rallied and managed to make it through that first winter. By midway through the following year, more than half of the Jews that had been deported with the Baers had also perished, most of them victims of the harsh conditions. Three hundred more were later exterminated, primarily at Auschwitz. All told, less than ten percent of the Jews on that September 15 transport from Frankfurt survived to liberation.

As the deportations continued, Nazi officials forcibly relocated all remaining Jews in Frankfurt to an ever-decreasing number of "collection homes" (*Sammelhäuser*), which they had commandeered in the eastern end of the city. Although the regime's primary intent was to free up scarce housing for non-Jewish residents, this policy had an important psychological effect as well. Though Frankfurt had never had a Jewish ghetto per se, the east end had historically been the most heavily Jewish area of the city. The actions of the Gestapo during the early 1940s had the effect of re-collecting the Jews of Frankfurt into the very same areas that their upwardly mobile parents and grandparents had chosen to migrate out of decades earlier. The result was a *de facto* re-partitioning of Frankfurt into Jewish and non-Jewish sections, even without the establishment of a formal walled-in ghetto.

By the end of 1942, the Gestapo had completed its program of large-scale deportations. In the eleven months beginning in November 1941, over eight thousand men, women and children from Frankfurt had either been sent to the concentration camps or simply murdered outright. In all, the Nazis deported over 11,000 thousand men, women and children from Frankfurt, almost 90 percent of whom, more than 9,500 Jews, ultimately lost their lives.

As 1943 approached, only a few scattered Jewish souls remained in the city. The vast majority of these people, like my grandmother, were protected spouses in mixed marriages who were still hoping to outlast the Nazi regime. My mother and her sister, though well aware that their Jewish relatives had been deported, were still too young to fully understand what had happened to the people they loved. Though suspicions were growing across the society as a whole, most ordinary Germans were not yet aware that their government was systematically exterminating the Jewish deportees. What little my grandparents did know about the concentration camps at that time, they chose not to share with their daughters. Still, in spite of the fact that they themselves were not yet directly threatened, Friedel and Selma were careful to remind their girls regularly never to talk with anyone outside the family about their situation. Only much later did my grandparents realize how much at risk they all had been during this time, protected mainly by the fact that the Gestapo, still operating from the membership lists confiscated from the Jewish Community, remained largely unaware of Selma's presence.

The Nazis spared a few others too, at least for a while. Bertha Marx, my grandmother's sister, was one of these. In late 1942 she was pregnant with her third child, and despite the fact that her husband Jakob was already in Theresienstadt, local authorities granted Bertha and her two boys a reprieve until after the new baby was born. In the meantime, the Gestapo moved the family into a *Sammelhaus*, where they could keep a better eye on the three of them.

Selma was permitted to visit her sister periodically, and sometimes she took Erika with her. My mother remembers vividly the last time she saw her aunt. It was March of 1943, and the new baby, Chana, had just been born. By Nazi edict, Jewish children could no longer have German names, so the infant was given a Hebrew one instead. The tiny infant lay swaddled in a laundry basket in her mother's room, a lone shock of her dark hair peeking out from among the bedclothes. The arrival of her new daughter should have been a happy event. Instead, it heralded the end of Bertha's protected status, and plans for the family's deportation were already underway.

Once again, with his wife's relatives threatened, my grandfather stepped to the fore. Karl Heinz, Bertha's oldest son, had a father who was not Jewish. Under the Nuremberg Laws, he could have been spared. My mother still has fond memories of her cousin Karl, who was renowned throughout the family as an avid practical joker, and who was, according to his grandmother Jenny, never without a smile on his face. Friedel pleaded with Bertha to leave the boy behind, promising his sister-in-law that he would care for her son as one of his own. It was true that both money and living space were quite limited in my grandparents' household, but what sufficed for the four of them could certainly be stretched to cover one more. Bertha, however, for all her faults, would not let herself be parted from her son. Not comprehending the danger that lay ahead, she followed her heart. "Where I go, my children go," she told my grandfather—a choice that would ultimately cost Karl Krauskopf his life.

"Frankfurt Hauptbahnhof ca. 1935"

On March 16, 1943, just two weeks after giving birth to Chana, Bertha, her sons Karl Heinz and Artur, ages thirteen and four, her new infant, and forty-one other Jews were taken to the main train station and loaded into a specially locked car at the back of a regular passenger train. In a way, they were fortunate. This latest group of deportees included a number of decorated WWI veterans, and in recognition of their earlier service to the Fatherland, the Gestapo had previously refrained from deporting these men. Now at least, they would be spared a direct trip to gas chambers of Auschwitz. Instead, the train took Bertha and the rest of the Frankfurt Jews first to Berlin, where they met up with small groups of Jews from other cities, before traveling onwards to join the thousands of others already at Theresienstadt.

Bertha and the children arrived at the camp on March 18 to find that Jenny, at least, was still alive. Whether Jakob Marx survived long enough to see his family again or not, we do not know. It must have been a bittersweet moment for all of them. At last, Jenny was no longer alone, but the knowledge of what lay ahead for all of them, including the new baby she was meeting for the first time, must have tempered any joy she felt. There are no witnesses who can tell us what Jenny said to her daughter that day she arrived, but by the time Bertha and the children came to Theresienstadt, Jenny had already endured more than seven months of concentration camp life, watching helplessly as countless others had died or been re-deported to the death camps. She surely would have known that not all of her precious grandchildren were likely to survive.

VI. THE FIRE

On June 16, 1943, Gestapo officials deported the last nineteen *Volljuden* from Frankfurt, cleansing the city of virtually all its Jewish inhabitants. After that, only about five hundred men and women remained of what was once, at its height of 30,000 members, the second largest Jewish population in Germany. Just ten years after seizing power, the Nazis had succeeded in destroying a Jewish Community that had thrived in Frankfurt for centuries.

Even for non-Jewish residents of the city, life had grown increasingly dangerous. British warplanes had begun bombing Frankfurt as far back as May 1941. Fortunately, there were few military targets in the mostly residential section where my grandparents lived. Nevertheless, as Allied forces progressively degraded German air defenses, the assaults occurred more and more frequently in almost every part of the city.

In the early months of the war, my mother's family had taken what shelter they could in the basement under their building. My grandparents' apartment, like most in Germany today, came with a narrow storage area below ground level. Friedel and Selma combined their cellar room with several of their neighbors', reinforcing the ceiling with extra wooden beams, to create a shelter of sorts. It was a makeshift arrangement at best, and one that afforded the occupants little chance of surviving a direct hit, but at least residents of the building had some protection from incendiary bombs and flying shrapnel. In the beginning, huddled underground with the sounds of the bombs exploding sometimes quite close by, the adults' greatest fear was that the roof would come crashing

93

down on their heads. For Erika and Inge Zins, however, there were much more important things to worry about. The cold, dark basement boasted a healthy population of rats, and my mother still shudders when she thinks of their furry little feet skittering across her lap in the darkness, often followed by the small sharp pain of something unseen nipping at her hand or thigh. As the raids became more common and the neighbors survived each successive attack, the adults' fear began to subside a bit. For my grandparents' two young daughters though, the terror provoked by their four-legged attackers never went away.

Not long after the bombings started, my grandfather joined the *Luftschutz*, a group of neighborhood air wardens responsible for maintaining order and safety among the civilian population during the attacks. This could be exceedingly dangerous work. On one occasion, an incendiary device landed on the building across the street from my grandparents' apartment but failed to detonate. None of the men were trained in handling explosives, but when no official help showed up, Friedel decided he had to act to protect his family and friends. He succeeded in retrieving the bomb without injury, later detonating it harmlessly in a nearby field. The bravery of my grandfather was beyond question. What would have happened, however, to my mother and the rest of her family had Friedel lost his life that night is anyone's guess.

As the frequency of the air raids rose, city officials constructed a series of hardened bunkers throughout Frankfurt to provide better protection for neighborhood residents. Some of these shelters still exist, and a few years ago, I went to look at the one in Praunheim where my mother's family usually took refuge. The huge, reinforced concrete, above ground structure fills an entire city block. Windowless cubicles, ten feet on a side, line the narrow hallways on each side of the five-story building. Nowadays, the locals use these spaces mostly for storage. A fledgling rock group even rents one of the rooms to practice in, so as not to disturb their neighbors. During the raids, however, two or three families wedged themselves into each tiny room. Although some of the locals tried to stake a claim to a particular space as their own, there were no official assignments and rooms usually filled on a first-come, first-served basis. Latecomers who tried to squeeze their way into an already over-crowded bunker often caused more than a little grumbling. Most of the bombings lasted between thirty minutes and two hours, though occasionally city officials would have to wait much longer before sounding the all clear. Later in the war, when several raids often took place in a single day, my mother and her sister and the rest of the residents of Praunheim often spent the majority of their day running back and forth between their apartments and the relative safety of the shelter.

"Praunheim bunker"

Rumor had it that even a direct hit could not bring down one of these massive structures, and one day my mother got a chance to see that claim tested first hand. She was out shopping in her grandparents' neighbor-hood in Bockenheim when the sirens went off. Almost simultaneously, the bombs began to fall. Quickly, Erika followed the locals to the nearest refuge. She thought she was safe, until a huge explosion rocked one end of the bunker, completely shearing off an entire corner of the building. For several ominous moments, the whole structure swayed from side to side. Many of those inside panicked, fearing a collapse, but eventually the shelter settled back firmly on its foundation. Erika escaped, shaken but unharmed.

Most of the air raids took place at night, and because he worked third shift, my grandfather would usually be away from home when the planes came. Before their mother's arrest, Erika and Inge at least had one adult to look after them during the bombings. After the Gestapo took Selma away, however, the two adolescents had to learn how to manage on their own.

Strict blackout conditions prevailed in Frankfurt throughout the war, but my grandfather always insisted that his daughters keep a single bulb burning to act as a signal. He taught the girls to let the bulb tell them what to do. If the light was still steady when the bombing began, then they probably had enough time to make a run for it. If, on the other hand, the bulb was already flickering, that meant that the bombs were falling too close to make it to the bunker. In that case, Erika and Inge were not to leave the building, but to seek shelter in the reinforced cellar below instead.

The two sisters slept in their parents' bed in an alcove off the living room, and always in their regular clothes in case they had to leave quickly. Next to the front door, each girl kept a backpack containing a change of clothes and a light snack. This was all my grandfather would allow his daughters to carry. Their neighbors often arrived at the bunker laden with heavy suitcases and boxes filled with their household treasures, but Friedel did not want his daughters bogged down as they fled. He didn't want them risking their lives over what few valuable possessions the family had.

Running for the bunker, my mother would take her younger sister by the hand, and the two of them would scurry across the wide avenue in front of their apartment. Rather than fighting the streaming hordes jamming the sidewalks, the youngsters opted for a more direct route, darting through the apartment house on the opposite side and along the dirt paths in back to where shelter stood, just beyond the garden plots behind the building.

One night, while rushing through the darkness to beat the bombs, Erika tripped and fell, bruising her knee badly and losing one of her shoes in the process. There was no time to stop and search, so she limped on to the bunker and promptly passed out in the doctor's office. When he returned home from work the next morning and heard the news, my grandfather was furious. Though he was relieved that the girls were safe, losing a shoe in the midst of wartime rationing was no small matter. He had no idea where they were going to find Erika a replacement.

Friedel hated waiting out the bombings at work, with no way of knowing whether his daughters were safe or not. He took some comfort in the fact that he had trained them well, and though they were not yet teenagers, the Zins girls knew what they had to do to survive. Once in a while, Friedel would ride back to the apartment to check on them, but with enemy planes buzzing overhead, it was usually much too dangerous to maneuver his bicycle through the blacked-out streets. On those few occasions when Friedel did make it home, he would have to pedal back to the factory after the assault to finish his shift. Production could not be allowed to lag and his employers tolerated no excuses. Most of the time, it was morning before my grandfather could get home and find out for sure that the girls were OK. As the war progressed, the bombings came so frequently that to Erika and Inge, the experience came to seem almost routine. For my mother and her sister, born just as the Nazis were coming to power, it was sometimes hard to remember a time when they hadn't been running for their lives on a daily basis.

In mid-1943, Nazi officials in Frankfurt consolidated remaining Jewish operations in Frankfurt at Hermesweg 5-7, a large three-story house originally erected by members of the *Jüdische Gemeinde* as a religious school. After taking over, the Gestapo used the Hermesweg facility as a place to hold Jews slated for deportation, mostly partners in mixed marriages who had lost their protected status through death or divorce of their non-Jewish spouse. The regime also set up a small infirmary on the site, ostensibly to provide care to Jews who, like my grandmother, had been banned from the city's hospitals. After seizing her from her hospital bed, it was to the Hermesweg infirmary that Gestapo officers initially took Selma in September of 1943.

Friedel returned home from his visit one day and sat his daughters down in front of him. He started to explain that the Nazis were going to take their mother away, probably for a long time. Inge cried. My mother remembers just feeling numb. The children knew that "taking away"—the same thing they had seen happen to the rest of their Jewish relatives—meant that they might never see their mother again. In spite of recent events, none of them had believed that this could really happen. Friedel's mother Maria, who had been helping around the house after Selma's arrest, was at the apartment when her son delivered the devastating news. Now, she grew angry with Erika for not seeming to be more upset, but Friedel jumped to his daughter's defense. "She'll cry when she's ready," he told his mother.

Except for a brief few days, Selma spent her first several weeks of house arrest inside the Hermesweg facility. At one point, thinking that she had finally recovered from her surgery, Nazi officials tried to move Selma to the city jail at Hammelsgasse, the top floor of which they had commandeered specifically for Jewish detainees. My grandmother wasn't there long, however, before she began suffering fainting spells—possibly due to the lingering effects of her operation, but more likely just a result of nervousness and stress. Or, maybe Selma even faked some of her symptoms to get out of her unhappy predicament. Whatever the true cause, she managed to convince her guards that she was not yet well enough to be mixed in with the general prison population, and before long, the Gestapo moved Selma back to the more comfortable surroundings at Hermesweg.

On the night of October 4, 1943, British and American bombers began the first of several major air campaigns against the city of Frankfurt. That night, the attackers focused their assault on the northern and eastern portions of the city, including the area where Selma was being held. Even from their location on the western fringe of the city, Friedel and the girls could hear the explosions off in the general direction of the collection house. Worried, the three of them climbed to the top floor of their building to try to get a better look. Even from several miles away, it was obvious that major fires had erupted in the streets surrounding Hermesweg. My grandfather didn't hesitate. Stashing Erika and Inge back in the apartment, he set out across the city on his bicycle, heading for the worst hit areas. Entering the bombed-out sections, Friedel picked his way through the rubble and broken glass, guided only by the light of the fires blazing around him. In recounting his journey to his daughters later that night, my grandfather marveled at having made it through unscathed, without even so much as a flat tire.

Rounding the corner onto Hermesweg, Friedel found the house at #5-7 already ablaze. Scanning the chaos in front of him, his eyes found Selma standing among a group of fellow prisoners across the street from the burning house. The women were all in their nightclothes and, at least for the moment, appeared to be unguarded.

As a rule, the Gestapo never permitted Jewish detainees to leave the building during the air raids, even as they routinely sought shelter for themselves in a nearby bunker. On the night of October 4, guards had initially locked the Jews inside the house as the bombs began to fall. Soon, however, it became obvious that the prisoners would surely burn alive if not allowed out, which was apparently too much even for local Nazi officials, at least at that point in time. By the time Friedel arrived, the guards were nowhere to be seen. Hurriedly, my grandparents discussed what to do. There would never be another chance like this, but

Selma could not just go back home again. The family's apartment was the first place the Gestapo would come looking for her, and such a blatant act of disobedience would surely result in swift and severe punishment. If she fled, she would have to go into hiding.

The reality was that my grandfather, a common laborer, had neither the money nor the political connections necessary to get his wife out of the city, and both of them knew it. Without a safe haven to run to, my grandparents could only stand on the street corner and watch, as the house where Selma had been held burned to the ground. When the bombing eventually ceased, Nazi guards rematerialized out of the darkness and rounded up their captives.

As he watched her being led away, Friedel swore to his wife that he would never let her be taken from him again, but he knew it was an empty promise. Selma's last chance to escape had vanished into the cool night air, like the smoke from the now-exhausted fire. When it was all over, my grandfather got on his bicycle and began to pedal back slowly through the darkened streets. He needed a little time to think before facing the inevitable questions from his daughters. He braced himself as Erika and Inge rushed to greet him at the door. "I had to give her back to them," was all he could say.

Gestapo agents took Selma and the rest of the prisoners to the sole remaining collection house in Frankfurt, at Ostendstrasse 18. There, Friedel could still visit periodically, and once a week he would bring the girls along to see their mother. Children were not permitted inside, so my grandfather bribed one of the *Kapos* (Jewish prisoners made to guard their fellow Jews) to bring his wife to a window at the front of the house. Standing on the opposite side of the wide, tree-lined street, Erika and Inge could at least exchange blown kisses with their mother and see that she was still okay.

The sudden influx of residents from Hermesweg caused severe overcrowding at the Ostendstrasse facility, prompting officials to step up the pace of deportations. It was not long before they decided that it was Selma's turn to go.

The girls never got the chance to say goodbye. A few days later, Friedel's sister-in-law, Maria, rushed into to the apartment to report that she had seen Selma being led to the train station by Gestapo officers with their dogs. The last time Erika and Inge had spoken to their mother was weeks earlier, just before the officers had taken her from her hospital bed at St. Elizabeth's. Friedel rushed down to the main station, but he was too late. Before he could get there, Selma was gone.

My grandfather never did understand why the Gestapo chose to move his wife out of Frankfurt when they did. He remained convinced throughout the war that her deportation had been a mistake, most likely resulting from all the confusion in the aftermath of the Hermesweg fire. Unbeknownst to him, despite the fact that the protected status of those in mixed marriages did not officially end until early 1944, plans to deport all Jews remaining in the Reich had been in place for some time. Hitler's men were moving cautiously, though, after an earlier attempt to break up the families of Aryan spouses in Berlin had provoked several days of civil unrest, eventually forcing the Gestapo to back down. As a concession to their non-Jewish spouses, and in a rare instance of restraint, the regime granted these final deportees a reprieve from immediate extermination at Auschwitz. The precise records of my grandmother's deportation no longer exist, but the best evidence suggests that the Gestapo included her with a group of seven Hungarian women, sent from the house at Ostendstrasse to the Ravensbrück concentration camp north of Berlin on October 29, 1943.

~:~

As a child, listening to my mother describe these events — Friedel bicycling through the bomb blasts to try to rescue his wife and, when that didn't work, trying once again to win her freedom by single-handedly confronting the Nazi bureaucracy in the citadel of its power; my grandfather's adventures sounded impossibly courageous. Looking back now, though, it's one of his lesser exploits that actually intrigues me more, particularly for what his actions have to say about the nature of heroism. No one forced my grandfather to go to Hermesweg the night of the fire or to Berlin several weeks later. These missions were fraught with danger, but in a way, they were also almost obligatory. The potential benefits were enormous, and there wasn't anyone besides Friedel who could possibly win Selma's release. His decision to serve as an air-raid warden, in contrast, strikes me as another matter entirely. As much as I admire my grandfather, I'm not sure I would have done the same thing in his place. Had he been killed as a member of the *Luftschutz*, either while defusing that unexploded bomb or in some other activity, the chances of his wife and children surviving the war would have plummeted. No doubt many of his neighbors could probably have made the same argument, but that doesn't change my belief that that was one particular job that could have, and probably should have, been left to others.

I don't know whether with each of his acts of heroism my grandfather ever stopped to consider how much danger he was putting himself and his family into. To some, his behavior might even appear reckless, but I don't see it that way. Heroism does not depend on circumstance and bravery cannot be turned on and off at will. As I've studied his life, I've come to realize that Friedrich Zins lived by a personal code that did not mutate in the face of expediency.

In his later years, one thing my grandfather spoke openly about was the guilt he could never shed for not having rescued his wife when he had the chance that night of the fire. I don't know if my grandparents ever discussed those events again between themselves, but if so neither of them ever told us what they had said to each other, standing on that street corner across from the burning collection house with no place to run. I suspect that it was just too painful, even after many years had passed, for Friedel to think about just how powerless he had been at that most critical moment in their lives.

VII. THERESIENSTADT AND AUSCHWITZ

Most people who haven't walked through a concentration camp may think they were all the same, but the reality is that each installation had its own peculiar characteristics and purpose in the Nazi system. Auschwitz was, infamously, a death factory. Ravensbrück, where my grandmother endured sixteen months of captivity, was primarily a work camp, though tens of thousands died there as well. Theresienstadt, the place where Hitler's men sent the rest of Selma's family, functioned as a city-sized holding pen, used by the Nazis as a staging ground for the onward deportation of Jews to the extermination camps of Poland.

In spring 2000, my mother and I flew to the Czech Republic to have a look for ourselves. I had been to the country once before briefly, just after the fall of Communism a decade earlier. In the intervening years, the capital of Prague had transformed itself from a dilapidated Cold War relic into a modern, westernized city. Workers had removed much of the ubiquitous grime of the Soviet era, and the downtown area, in addition to its spectacular architecture, now sported a healthy collection of famous-name stores as well.

We made our way north out of the city in our rented *Skoda*, and I quickly realized that the rest of the country was still waiting to enjoy the benefits of freedom. Villages along the way appeared strikingly colorless — suffused with the blacks and grays that had been so characteristic of life behind the Iron Curtain. It was the middle of the day, but in each small town we passed, large numbers of working-aged men idled on the street corners.

An hour or so and a couple of wrong turns later (my knowledge of Czech road signs being somewhat limited), we approached Theresienstadt, now once again referred to by its Czech name of Terezin. Passing through the outskirts of the town, we drove past an imposing military installation remarkable for the row upon row of Jewish graves stretching out from in front of the main gate, each marked with a six-pointed star. Apart from the oddly misnamed Small Fortress, as the structure is known, Terezin appears nowadays to be a very ordinary place. Nondescript buildings surround a large central square, and local inhabitants amble about their business in no particular hurry. An unmistakable air of sleepiness pervades the place.

"Terezin Central Square 2003"

The City of Theresienstadt, founded by the German Kaiser Josef II and named for his mother Maria Theresia, lies in the heart of the *Sudetenland*, a disputed region in the northeastern corner of the Czech Republic that Germany controlled until 1918. After seizing power in 1933, Hitler wasted no time in reclaiming sovereignty over the region, ostensibly to protect the safety of the large numbers of ethnic Germans still living there. Nazi troops invaded in March of 1938, meeting with little local resistance. The resulting international uproar prompted the now-infamous Munich Conference later that year. During the enclave, the British and French governments (the Czechs were conspicuously not invited) acquiesced to Hitler's aggression, having mistakenly convinced themselves that appeasing the German leader would be the best way to prevent a wider war.

A series of earthen walls, originally constructed to ward off 18th-century Prussian invaders from the north, surrounds the town itself. Theresienstadt thus provided the Nazis with the perfect location to incarcerate their victims. Hitler's men seized upon the idea that this protective bastion, isolated and easily guarded, would be uniquely useful in hemming in the Jews.

The regime worked hard to maintain the fiction that being sent to Theresienstadt was a privilege, all the while knowing that the ultimate intent was to transport the Jews onward to the mass extermination camps farther east. Deportees and residents initially lived side-by-side, although German officials had strictly forbidden the Jews from interacting with the locals. As time went on, guards placed additional restrictions on the prisoners' movements. Prior to its conversion into a concentration camp, approximately 3,500 people had lived in the town of Terezin, including about five hundred ethnic Germans mixed in with the majority Czechs. By June 1942, however, the Nazis had forcibly resettled the last of the original inhabitants. After that, prisoner transports began to arrive more frequently, sometimes two or three times per day, each one usually carrying more than a thousand deportees.

Trains carrying Jews to Theresienstadt terminated in the neighboring town of Bauschowitz, the location of the nearest station. Sick or handicapped prisoners, like Selma's stepfather Berthold Baer, were loaded into trucks on the platform. The rest marched the two and a half kilometers to the front of the camp, dragging their personal possessions along with them, only to surrender whatever items of value they still possessed immediately upon passing through the gates. New prisoners then received their work assignment. Unlike at other camps, there was very little outside industry at Theresienstadt, so most inmates worked either in camp maintenance, food production, or at the hospital.

By September 1942, the Nazis had crammed over 53,000 Jews into a town that had held less than one-tenth as many inhabitants before the war. New inmates quickly became indoctrinated into the harshness of concentration camp life. Fleas and bedbugs plagued every building, lines for the latrines stretched interminably, and epidemics of disease erupted repeatedly. Each prisoner was allotted only a miniscule four-by-four foot patch of living space — to be used for eating, sleeping, storage of personal items, and everything else. The Nazis were not about to waste resources on those they planned to exterminate, so they limited food rations severely. The amount of nourishment a prisoner received depended on his or her ability to be useful. Prisoners who could do the hardest labor received 500 grams (about a pound) of food per day — fully 50 percent more than those who were able to do no work at all. Meals, often served cold, usually consisted of a cup of ersatz coffee in the morning, a bowl of watery soup along with a single thin slice of bread at lunch, and perhaps some soup again at the end of the day. Once a week, if he or she were lucky, each prisoner also received a dumpling. Survival depended crucially upon finding ways to supplement these meager official rations. Many prisoners bartered with kitchen workers for extra food; others simply stole whatever they could from other inmates. Inevitably, fights broke out; altercations that the Nazi guards encouraged, believing correctly that infighting among the prisoners would only undermine any organized attempts at resistance.

Faced with such hardships, Berthold Baer never had a chance. He died on October 3, 1942, less than three weeks after arriving in Theresienstadt. The sudden loss must have devastated Jenny, who had kept hoping for so long that her stricken husband would somehow recover.

VII. THERESIENSTADT AND AUSCHWITZ

She hadn't yet had the time to develop the kind of support network among fellow inmates that was often crucial during such times of crisis, and now, except for her son-in-law Jakob, Jenny was completely alone. Still, drawing perhaps on what was left of her youthful willfulness, she refused to let herself succumb to her despair.

To make room for the constant flow of new arrivals, camp administrators issued quotas for the numbers and categories of prisoners to be re-deported. It was this constant threat of being sent to the East that hovered over every aspect of camp life. The Nazi-appointed Council of Elders was charged with selecting the specific individuals who had to go. Council members were well aware of the fate of those they sent away, and many survivors have criticized these men for their apparent complicity with their Nazi overlords, but it is also true that Nazi guards stood ready to step in and make the selections themselves if the Jewish leaders refused to cooperate. Despite their apparent power over life and death, virtually all of the Elders (along with their entire families) were also eventually sent to their deaths. Nazi officials went to great lengths to conceal what would happen to the deportees, but gradually the truth began to seep out. Avoiding having one's name placed on the list grew to be the major challenge of camp life, and survival depended on being able to distinguish oneself in some way from the anonymous masses targeted for extermination. Working in some essential capacity, such as providing medical care to other inmates, provided the best insurance. Jenny Baer, unfortunately, had no such skills to offer.

Despite the regime's best efforts to control information, stories about the treatment of the Jews in Nazi concentration camps began leaking to the outside world as well. In February 1943, responding to international political pressure, Hitler's men temporarily halted transports from Theresienstadt to Auschwitz. At about this same time, representatives of the International Red Cross pressured the German government for the right to inspect conditions in the camps, ultimately securing an agreement to make a site visit in the spring of the following year.

The regime responded with an elaborate program of preparations. In Theresienstadt, beginning in the summer of 1943 and extending into the early part of 1944, prisoners cleaned and repainted the buildings while Nazi officials went about sanitizing the camp's image. Administrators reclassified the town from a ghetto to a *Jüdisches Siedlungsgebiet*, or "Jewish Residential District." The *Lagerkommandantur*, or Camp Headquarters became the *Dienststelle*, or "Service Center." Streets were given new and more pleasant-sounding names such as *Seestrasse* (despite the fact that there was no lake or sea visible from the town), *Bahnhof-strasse* (though Theresienstadt had no train station) and *Parkstrasse* (even as Jews remained forbidden to enter the town's parks). Officials created a new camp currency, and a coffee house (whose menu consisted of but a single item — ersatz coffee) opened on the main street. The coffee house was the also only place in Theresienstadt where prisoners could actually use the new "money" that their Nazi masters had so generously provided to them. Over the summer, circus tents sprouted on the town square, camp directors relaxed an earlier ban on the organizing of concerts and theater performances, and inmates even formed a soccer team — and all the while Jews continued to starve to death on a daily basis. In May, the Nazis culled any emaciated or ill-appearing inmates from the camp populations, disposing of such undesirables out of sight of the international community. There was one redeeming feature in the midst of all this cynical image making: the institution of a temporary moratorium on the re-deportation of children to the death camps, my mother's three young cousins included. The Nazis apparently believed (rightly so, as it turned out) that the presence of children would assist the regime in putting a better face forward for the world.

With their preparations completed, Nazi officials commissioned the making of a film entitled *The City the Fuhrer Gave the Jews*, which, among other appealing images of camp life, depicted bucolic scenes of Jewish children playing happily in the newly spruced up town. The final portion of the movie recorded a performance of the children's opera *Brundibär*, written by a Jewish inmate of Theresienstadt. True to form, shortly after the filming ended, the Nazis sent most of the children who had acted and sung in the production to Auschwitz to be gassed. Around the world today, Jewish groups occasionally still perform *Brundibär*, in remembrance of those who were lost. The original propaganda film, so successful at deceiving the world, has been preserved as part of the permanent memorial collection at Yad Vashem in Israel.

As the time for the Red Cross visit drew closer, Nazi leaders began to fear that Theresienstadt alone, no matter how well presented, might not be enough to convince the world of their benevolent intentions. To help bolster their case, officials decided to spruce up a section of the main camp at Auschwitz as well. In September of 1943, the initial group of deportees to this new area, confusingly designated as the Theresienstadt *Familienlager* ("Family Camp") — also known as Birkenau BIIb — was spared immediate selection to the gas chambers. Instead, guards took the prisoners directly to the Family Camp where, ironically, they promptly split up the men, women, and children and sent them to separate barracks separated by wire fences. To make the *Familienlager* seem as appealing as possible to the inspectors, the Nazis granted the Jews in Birkenau BIIb certain "privileges" not available to the general population at Auschwitz. The prisoners' hair was not shorn, rations were somewhat better for a while, and closets were installed for inmates to store their meager personal belongings. Prisoners were also permitted to send letters to friends and relatives once every fourteen days, and to receive occasional packages from outside the camp. Workers even went so far as to construct a small garden for the children to play in. Incredibly, all of this took place within full view of the smoke pouring from the chimneys of Auschwitz' four crematoriums.

On December 16, 1943, an additional 2,500 Jews from Theresienstadt arrived at the Family Camp. Despite the marginally improved conditions, Jews in the special section continued to die at an appalling rate. By the beginning of March 1944, over eleven hundred residents of Birkenau BIIb had succumbed due to "natural causes." Then, on the night of March 8, with the Red Cross visit still three months away, the Nazis gassed virtually all remaining residents of the *Familienlager*. Over the next few weeks, three new groups of Jews from Theresienstadt arrived to take their place. My great-grandmother, Jenny Baer, was part of this fresh contingent. She arrived at Auschwitz on May 16, 1944, aboard Transport "Dz."

On June 23, 1944, the Red Cross delegation, under the direction of Dr. Maurice Rossel, inspected both Theresienstadt and the *Familienlager* at Auschwitz. From the Nazis' point of view, the visit went very well indeed. During interviews afterward with the international press, Dr. Rossel gushed in praise of the conditions he had observed. Newspapers worldwide published photos of Jewish children playing in the streets and parks of Theresienstadt. On the very same day as Dr. Rossel's visit, however, the International Red Cross also received a published report based on the statements of two men who had earlier escaped from Auschwitz. In their account, the former prisoners described in detail how the Nazis systematically exterminated large numbers of Jews at that installation. Unconcerned over the stark contrast between the experiences of these men and the conditions observed by their own inspectors, Red Cross officials chose to ignore the testimony of those who had personally witnessed the Nazi death apparatus in action, and the world's attention quickly moved on to other issues.

Although exact records of her fate do not exist, Jenny Baer most likely lived for several weeks after her arrival in Auschwitz, awaiting the Red Cross visit with the rest of her doomed companions in the *Familienlager*. After Dr. Rossel and his entourage departed, with the Potemkin-like façade having served its purpose so admirably, the regime moved quickly to liquidate the separate camp. In early July, the infamous Dr. Josef Mengele selected the most able-bodied young men and women for transfer to forced labor battalions. Then, on July 10, guards staged a general arrest in the Family Camp. Three thousand women and children were promptly gassed. Another raid occurred the following day and the rest of the survivors, roughly 4,000 men, women and children, were also promptly put to death. My great-grandmother almost certainly perished in one of those two final groups.

Soon thereafter, the program of regular deportations from Theresienstadt to Auschwitz resumed. Between September 9 and October 28, 1944, the Nazis sent over 18,000 Jews to Auschwitz to be exterminated. Bertha Marx and her three children arrived on October 18 and were immediately sent to the gas chambers. Their bodies were taken to Crematorium III for disposal. By the end of October 1944, out of a population that had once reached almost 60,000 souls, only 11,000 Jews remained alive in Theresienstadt.

"Only known surviving image of Bertha Marx (front row, fifth from right — seen here at Friedel and Selma's engagement party)"

When I finally made my own pilgrimage to see the extermination factory at Auschwitz-Birkenau, I found it difficult to grasp the inconceivable vastness of the place. At the front of the camp stands the former Commandant's Headquarters, that building made infamous around the world by pictures of the single train track running through the arched opening at its center. Upstairs, looking out of the second-story windows of what is now a small museum, it's almost impossible to make out the perimeter of the camp in the distance. Inside the fences, outlines of the countless rows of prisoner barracks imprint the ground to this day. At the back of the camp lie the remains of Auschwitz' four major crematoriums, dynamited by the Nazis as they fled the Soviet advance in early 1945 in a failed attempt to destroy the evidence of their crimes. A sea of tiny flags, each bearing a blue and white Star of David, dots the ruins — left there by the multitudes that have come to pay their respects.

"Ruins of Crematorium, with flags"

Each of these Nazi factories of death had an entrance but no exit. Guards herded the condemned down several steps, through a door at the rear and into the supposed shower chamber, where the prisoners were made to undress. After the gassings, when the screams had all died down and the room had been cleared of its poisonous vapors, other Jewish prisoners carried fresh corpses by the hundreds to the ovens in the front room. To say that visiting this site is disturbing would be to state the obvious, but seeing all this with my own eyes troubled me in ways I had not anticipated — quite apart from the horror of the mass exterminations themselves. I've always admired the German penchant for efficiency, a quality I observed in my grandparents and one I sought to emulate when I was a boy. Here, however, was an example of that vaunted efficiency twisted in the most grotesque way imaginable. It was deeply disquieting to think that the Nazis had taken a trait that I admired so highly and used it to produce so much evil.

~:~

In the nearly four years of its existence, over 140,000 Jews passed through the Theresienstadt concentration camp. Of those, more than 87,000 were re-deported to the extermination camps at Riga, Minsk, and Auschwitz. The fortunate ones perished en route. Most of the rest, including all of my grandmother's immediate family, were put to death — the vast majority at Auschwitz. Of all those sent to the east, only 3,600 were still alive at the time of Europe's liberation.

Survivors of the Holocaust have often referred to Theresienstadt as the "City of Lies." Everything there was untrue: from Hitler's promise to make a gift of the city, to the worthless camp currency, to the empty building façades and other illusions created for the Red Cross investigation. Today, Theresienstadt is once again the sleepy Czech village it once was. Little remains to remind residents or visitors of the Nazi period, and most of the people who now live in the town are too young to remember the atrocities that took place there during the war years. Next to the main square sits a pale yellow, unobtrusive-looking building, home to a museum detailing Terezin's Nazi past. The display inside is dry and unimpressive, except for a series of marble slabs mounted along the wall of one room. On them, etched forever in stone, are the names of all the children who passed through the camp, including those of my three small cousins.

"Theresienstadt Wall of Names"

I have to confess now that I when I first heard my mother tell me the stories about her relatives who had died in the concentration camps, I felt strangely unmoved. I was only a child myself then, and the names of all these people were only that — just names alone, without any connection to the human beings that had been once called by them.

On the day we visited Theresienstadt, I stood staring at those inscriptions on the wall for quite a long time: Karl Heinz Krasukopf, the fun-loving prankster, Artur Marx, his impish little half-brother, and the infant Chana, who had known no life other than that of the concentration camp. After a decade of my life spent searching for their stories, I finally grasped the enormity of what Hitler and his men had stolen from my family and so many others. My little cousins had suffered unimaginably here, along with the tens of thousands of others, before being sent to Auschwitz to be gassed out of existence. If not for the crimes of the Nazis, those three innocent souls would probably still be alive today, and I would have known them myself. Instead, sixty years later, all that remains of my cousins' lives are my mother's fading memories and a few names on the wall of an obscure museum halfway around the world.

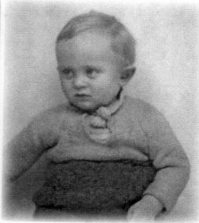

*"Karl Heinz Krauskopf and his
little brother Artur 'Addi' Marx in early 1940"*

VIII. RAVENSBRÜCK

Standing there in front of the camp, the view was serene. Off in the distance, I could just make out the picturesque eastern German village of Fürstenberg, its misty church spire and mosaic of brightly colored houses reflecting off the still waters of the lake at my feet. I realized early on in my quest to investigate my grandparents' story that I would have to come here, to see for myself the place where my grandmother had endured a year and a half of the worst deprivation and punishment one human being can inflict on another. Now, gazing out over that incongruously tranquil vista, with the concrete walls of the Ravensbrück concentration camp rising just behind me, it was hard to grasp the evil that had enveloped this place so many years before.

As a child, I had always been a little afraid to talk to my grandmother about her time in the concentration camp, for fear of upsetting whatever presumably delicate accommodation she had made with her past. As far as I know, she never spoke with anyone else about it either. Right after the war, most survivors were not yet ready to talk about what had happened to them, and by the time many of them were, often not until years later, the world had largely moved on. In the hustle and bustle of post-war rebuilding, few people were interested. By the time I began my own research in the mid 1990s — more than a decade after my grandmother had died — I had to seek out other sources. Gradually, by talking with other survivors who had been at Ravensbrück during that same period and by studying published first-person accounts, I've been able to piece together what my grandmother's life in the camp must have been like. One woman's story in particular stood out: a small, thin little book entitled *Vom KZ ins Kloster (From Concentration Camp to Cloister)*, written by Katharina Katzenmeier, who entered the convent after having been a companion of Selma's during their escape together in the waning days of the war. Alas, I only discovered Frau Katzenmeier's book a few months after she, too, had passed away.

"Tranquil vista — the view from Ravensbrück across
Lake Schwedt to the village of Fürstenburg"

At first, it was just my mother and I who were going to make the pilgrimage to Ravensbrück, but after we announced our plans, one-by-one my siblings all called to say that they wanted to come along too. Until then, I hadn't thought about how deeply my grandparents' story must have affected their lives as well. A few weeks later, I slid our rented van in between the tour buses disgorging their throngs of schoolchildren in front of the camp gates and our little troupe spilled out. The students were all bubbly and excited to be out of the classroom for the day, though for us, of course, this was the most solemn of occasions. Still, I felt reassured to see that someone was attempting to teach these young Germans about their country's past. We hesitated for a moment, none of us quite sure what we were about to discover. I shot my mother an inquiring glance. "Are you sure you really want to do this?" I asked her with my eyes. Finally, we meandered up to the front gate.

Years before I embarked on this project, my mother and I had traveled together to the concentration camp at Dachau, near Munich. The Dachau memorial had seemed to me then a bit too sanitized, as if the German penchant for neatness and orderliness had somehow obscured the full horror of what took place there. Not so with Ravensbrück. Neglected for decades under the Communists, the ruins of Ravensbrück still echo that installation's bleak and hideous past. Most of the site consists only of scattered foundations now, marking the places where the overstuffed prisoners' barracks and SS factories filled with slave laborers once stood. Only a few buildings remain: the former Commandant's headquarters, now a museum and archive; the so-called Punishment Block, where Nazi guards tortured and starved those who had the audacity to violate their rules, and the small, square, nondescript crematorium, its inno-cent-looking chimney now long since mercifully silent.

We arrived at Ravensbrück on a raw day in early March. A cold, inter-mittent rain whipped out of somber grey skies, the kind of weather that makes you want to zip your coat up as high as it will go. As I stood in the large open space behind the Commandant's Headquarters where the twice-daily assemblies had taken place and watched the water beat down on the smoothly-tiled floor to my left (all that now remains of the former shower room), I thought about my grandmother and her fellow inmates, forced to endure the endless roll calls in the middle of the German winter without benefit of warm clothing. Suddenly, it wasn't so hard to imagine the fear and misery that enveloped the pris-oners every day of their lives at Ravensbrück.

~:~

The Ravensbrück Concentration Camp for Women opened in 1938, built by five hundred forced laborers imported from nearby Sachsenhausen. Hitler's men chose the location, some eighty kilometers north of Berlin, primarily for its excellent road and rail connections to the rest of the Reich. The virgin meadows and woods bordering the quiet village of Fürstenberg also offered abundant natural boundaries — the unspoiled Lake Schwedt on the west, a large forested area to the north and east, and the River Havel to the south. Initially, the camp consisted of fourteen wooden barracks for housing prisoners, two additional buildings for the Revier, or sick bay, a communal kitchen, an in-processing building with shower room and adjacent roll call grounds, and a detention block — all surrounded by twelve-foot-high concrete walls topped with barbed wire. Over time, workers added more buildings until eventually, Ravensbrück grew to be the second largest camp for women in the entire Nazi penal system (trailing only the infamous extermination factory at Auschwitz-Birkenau).

My grandmother's journey to Ravensbrück was both arduous and prolonged. Several times after leaving Frankfurt, she found herself imprisoned in cities along the way, standard procedure for the small groups then being deported by the Gestapo. At each stop, guards marched the prisoners through the city streets in full view of local inhabitants, before locking them up for the night in the local jail. Occasionally, a few of the bolder souls among the Jews would shout at passers-by, their protests of innocence most often falling unheeded. In spite of their predicament, the deportees did occasionally encounter surprising acts of kindness — a bystander offering to share a bit of food or a sympathetic guard willing to mail a letter home to loved ones. Most of the time, however, prisoners like my grandmother trudged along in silence, unable to see beyond their own misery and hopelessness.

Some of the stops lasted only a single night, but interruptions of a week or more were also commonplace. Frequently, Nazi guards threw the deportees into prison cells right alongside violent criminals, many of whom preyed on the relatively defenseless Jews. Conditions in the jails varied from tolerable to primitive. By far the worst were in the city of Halle, where guards packed as many as 150 women into a single small cell. Prisoners stood shoulder-to-shoulder all through the day and night, and no food or water was given. As uncomfortable as their extended trip often was, though, none of the deportees had any real sense of the much harsher fate that awaited them.

Several weeks after leaving Frankfurt, Selma arrived in the southeastern German city of Leipzig, a major industrial and transportation hub for the Third Reich. There, the Gestapo had collected deportees from various points of origin and reassembled them into larger groups for transport onwards to their final destinations. Because of its strategic significance, Leipzig had also become a favorite target of Allied bombers. On the night of October 20, 1943, just before my grandmother's arrival, a massive air attack destroyed the series of makeshift wooden barracks that the Nazis had been using as a transit camp. Scrambling to find an alternative, Gestapo officers quickly commandeered a portion of the city jail. As a result, shortly after coming to Leipzig, Selma once again wound up behind bars in the local prison.

Life in the Leipzig facility was bearable at first, if not particularly comfortable. There was shelter from the elements at least, and the food was usually adequate, but most of the prisoners had to sleep on the cold floor without mattresses or blankets. It didn't last for long. As additional deportees flooded in, the prison became more and more overcrowded and conditions deteriorated rapidly.

Selma had been in Leipzig for only a short time when Allied planes struck again. Code named "Operation Haddock," three hundred bombers took off from England on the night of December 3, turned southeast over Berlin, and arrived at Leipzig in successive waves between 3:50 and 4:25 AM. For the deportees, locked inside their cells as sirens screamed and bombs exploded around them, the attack was beyond terrifying. For Selma especially, the sounds of that night must have brought back unwelcome memories of being trapped inside of the burning house at Hermesweg just a few weeks earlier.

Unable to flee during the assault, the prisoners became frantic. In response, the guards beat them, trying to force the women to settle down. Finally, at 5:32 AM, local officials gave the all clear, but not before the Allies had dropped some 1,400 tons of bombs, killing over 1,100 people and wounding more than 3,000 others. The destruction was massive. The city's central business district, including the world-renowned Publisher's Quarter containing over 2 million books, had been obliterated. Most streets were impassable, power outages were widespread, and over 2,300 major fires blazed throughout the city.

Damages to the prison were less extensive, but some areas had become uninhabitable, meaning that the deportees crowded into an even smaller remaining space. Making matters worse yet, the attack had also disrupted rail connections to and from the city, delaying the onward movement of Jewish prisoners to the camps. Selma and her companions endured several additional weeks locked in their cells while repairs to the tracks took place.

One day in late December, the inevitable summons arrived. Nazi officers took Selma and thirty-seven other prisoners down to the main train station and locked them into specially modified railcars. Rumors had circulated for weeks that most deportees were being sent to a place called Ravensbrück, but few of the women had ever heard that name before, and none of them had any idea what to expect once they got there. As the train crept northwards, it wound its way directly through the heart of the Nazi empire in Berlin. Peering out the windows, the prisoners were shocked at what they saw. Nothing they had witnessed in Leipzig could compare to the extent of the destruction that stretched throughout the German capital in every direction. Later, as evening approached, the transport chugged into the station at Fürstenburg, the nearest stop to the camp. The Nazis liked to have new inmates arrive at night whenever possible, knowing that the darkness would only enhance the fear and disorientation that all new inmates faced. As the locomotive eased to a stop, SS guard dogs, snarling and barking, encircled the train cars. Lights flooded the platform, blinding the women as the guards prodded them down the steps. All around them, uniformed men shouted—"*Raus! Raus! Juden raus!*"

Leaving the station, the women marched through the streets of Fürstenburg as local residents gaped at them in silence. Four kilometers farther on, the prisoners approached the entrance to the camp. Loudspeakers mounted high atop the twelve foot high walls blasted commands: "*Marsch! Marsch! Lauf oder Stirb! Arbeit macht frei!*" ("March! March! Run or die! Work makes one free!).

"*Entrance to Ravensbrück as it appears today*"

As they neared the gates of the camp, the deportees were struck by the contrast between the picture postcard village they had just passed through and the forbidding compound they were about to enter. Even after the weeks of captivity, the sense of unreality about the whole experience sapped the women's will to resist. This was, of course, exactly what their Nazi captors had intended. On December 22, 1943, my grandmother and the rest of her fellow prisoners passed through the gates of hell, officially known as the Ravensbrück Concentration Camp.

As Selma entered the camp on that cold night three days before Christmas, the concrete walls of Ravensbrück engulfed her, severing all contact with the life she had known before. Guards herded the prisoners past soldiers lounging comfortably in the SS canteen on their left and on through the grounds into a large entry hall, where the women were immediately ordered to relinquish any personal items they still held. Camp rules banned all personal possessions except a toothbrush. Workers made a show of carefully cataloguing these confiscated goods — a ruse used to justify the theft of any valuables the SS thought they could sell for profit. My grandmother slipped the wedding band from her ring finger and passed it to the guard in front of her. It was the last time she would ever see her most prized possession.

"Twelve foot high walls surrounded the camp"

For the new arrivals, holding on to anything at all that reminded them of their former lives often provided a critical psychological boost. Many of the women smuggled small items into the camp, though this could be far more trouble than it was worth. Contraband possessions had to be kept out of the view of the guards at all times — a virtual impossibility given the close quarters and frequent inspections. Being found with forbidden goods was punishable by torture and solitary confinement, and, depending on the captors' mood at the time, could also result in summary execution. Even when they were not discovered, prisoners had to divert critical energies towards protecting their things from fellow inmates desperate for anything of value that could be traded for food.

After systematically looting the women of everything they owned, Nazi guards made the new inmates stand for several more hours, their resistance waning as they waited through the night for the arrival of the morning shift. When processing resumed, guards ordered the prisoners to remove their clothing and fold all items carefully at their feet. Next, they led the women into the shower room and sprayed them with ice cold water in a mock delousing. To complete the procedure, workers then shaved all of the prisoners' hair from their bodies, making no effort to clean the razors between inmates. In their rush to complete their task, guards took little care to avoid injury. Not only were the women traumatized psychologically, many were left physically bleeding as well. Finally, non-medical personnel probed the inmates' body cavities, still looking for valuables to confiscate. Once again, instruments were not disinfected from one exam to the next.

Hustled back outside naked and shivering into the cold winter air, each woman received a packet containing a striped dress made of rough cloth, a single pair of socks and a pair of wooden shoes. This was all the clothing that prisoners would have, day and night, winter and summer, without washing, for the duration of their stay in Ravensbrück. In later months, after the supply of new uniforms had run out, guards simply reissued the civilian clothing they had confiscated from earlier arrivals, but only after painting a large crude "X" across the back of each piece to identify the wearer as an inmate in the event of escape. Along with her prison garb, each woman received a dark red bowl, used for taking the meager soup that was to make up the majority of their diet. Since losing this one item was tantamount to a death sentence, many of the new inmates took to wearing their bowls on their heads for safekeeping.

Completing the intake process, each woman received a cloth number and one or more colored triangles to sew onto the sleeves of her camp dress. The colors indicated the reason for the bearer's presence at Ravensbrück — red for political prisoners; green for common criminals; purple for Jehovah's Witnesses; black for the so-called "Asocials" (a fluid designation used by the Nazis to justify the imprisonment of anyone they considered "undesirable"); and yellow, of course, for the Jews. These group designations were critical to one's chances of survival. Each prisoner's treatment and privileges depended on which group she belonged to. The SS tended to favor the Asocials, whom they viewed as at least technically part of the Aryan race, often placing them in positions of authority over the other prisoners. The Jews, in contrast, were always treated poorly — squeezed into the most overcrowded barracks, provided with the poorest rations, and subjected to the most backbreaking work assignments.

With the issuance of the number patches, the process of dehumanizing the prisoners was complete. My grandmother became simply Ravensbrück inmate #25753. As a concession to her Aryan husband, Selma had received an additional red triangle to wear over her Jewish yellow one. This was no trivial distinction. Every one of the former inmates I've talked to has insisted that my grandmother would not have survived for long without that additional designation. As a political prisoner, her captors saw her as different from the large group of her fellow Jews who languished at the bottom of the camp hierarchy.

After the new prisoners completed their in-processing, guards led them to Blocks 12 and 13, where the women would spend the next six weeks in quarantine, strictly segregated from their fellow prisoners and exempt even from the twice daily assemblies. Various epidemics had repeatedly ravaged Ravensbrück, and given the unavoidably close contact between the inmates and their minders, camp officials constantly feared that new outbreaks of contagious disease would spread to themselves and their families.

Each numbered block consisted of two sleeping chambers attached through a central dayroom, originally intended as a common area where prisoners could take their meals. By the time Selma arrived in late 1943, however, the sleeping rooms were already literally stuffed to the rafters, and the day areas had long since been converted to additional sleeping quarters. Barracks that had originally been designed to hold 300 women now routinely housed over 1,000 prisoners each. Stacks of bunks stood three tiers high, with five beds lashed together as a unit to increase stability. Four women slept in each bed, arrayed head-to-toe, or in whatever other configuration they could find to achieve some modicum of comfort. The military bedrolls given to prisoners in the early days of *Ravensbrück* had also disappeared by 1943, so there were few pillows or blankets to be had. There was also no heat. In the wintertime, it was so cold inside the sleeping chambers that icicles commonly hung from the ceiling.

Most blocks sported various infestations of lice, fleas and cockroaches, all of which were capable of transmitting disease with their bites. Healthy populations of mice and rats also roamed the prisoners' quarters. There was a constant battle among the inmates for the upper bunks, as those condemned to sleep below found themselves rained on by an unholy mixture of trash, bugs and bodily fluids.

Inside each block, a small bathroom contained a single large trough for all prisoners to wash in. Soap was nonexistent, most of the time there was no running water, and personal hygiene became impossible. The toilets consisted of a series of round holes cut in a long plank. Often it was many days before new arrivals adjusted to relieving themselves in such a public setting. Worse yet, the toilets stopped up frequently due to the overcrowding, and the stench of human waste permeated constantly throughout the barracks.

Those first few weeks in quarantine were a vulnerable time for most new inmates. Most were confused and homesick, and some were already seriously ill. Access to medical care for the prisoners was minimal. In spite of the fact that they were crowded in with as many as 50,000 other prisoners, many of the women at Ravensbrück felt hopelessly alone, as if no one on the outside would ever know where they were or what had happened to them. Gradually, of necessity, new bonds began to form between inmates — not just friendships but unique relationships that would endure through the worst of times. A silent grasp of the hand in a moment of crisis, a little support under the arm during the hours-long assemblies, the dabbing of lips parched with fever, or the finding of just one more little piece of bread somewhere to stave off starvation — these were all among the ways that the women of Ravensbrück tried to help each other to go on.

My grandmother had such a relationship, one that later played a critical role in saving her life. After several months of interminable work shifts and constant hunger, punctuated by several attacks of the dysentery that regularly swept through the camp, Selma had lapsed into a state of intense despair. Things had gotten so bad that she decided she could endure the pain no longer. A quick death had come to seem infinitely preferable to the ongoing miseries of starvation and slave labor. Selma decided to throw herself into the electrified fence that surrounded the factory where she worked. I don't know if she told her companion about her plans or not, but somehow my grandmother's friend found out about what she had in mind and managed to talk her through her hopelessness, convincing Selma to hang on just a little bit longer. Others who had no such support were not as lucky. More than a few prisoners, unable to see any other way out, did ultimately succeed in taking their own lives.

(After the war, Selma's companion — sadly, her name has not survived the years — came to visit my grandparents at their home in Frankfurt. On that day, perhaps for a moment, my grandfather may have glimpsed the nature of one of the remarkable partnerships spawned by concentration camp life. Isolated and vulnerable, the women of Ravensbrück found their own ways to survive. As far as I know, my grandmother never saw her friend and savior again, but it would not have mattered. The bond between these two women, forged in the midst of the chaos that was Ravensbrück, could never again be broken.)

After six weeks in quarantine, all new prisoners received their initial work assignments and were released into the main prisoner population. Still not fully realizing what lay ahead, many of the women longed to be relieved of the stifling boredom and put to work. Jobs located indoors in camp operations were the most coveted, especially those involving food preparation, which offered the inmates a chance to supplement their meager rations on the sly. Such opportunities were few, however, and most of the women wound up assigned instead to the SS factories at the back of the compound.

The SS industries were critical to making Ravensbrück a viable enterprise for the Nazis. The SS operated a sewing factory, a furrier shop, and a weaving and knitting facility that made reed mats and shoes, among other enterprises. There was also a large, open-air enclosure where prisoners sorted through the material confiscated from new arrivals, searching for items that German soldiers could use in the field or that the SS could sell for profit. In 1942 alone, over 5,000 prisoners working in the SS factories at Ravensbrück generated profits of 1.2 million marks for their masters, money that the Nazis used to fund the overall workings of the camp. By 1944, with mechanization enabling an increased pace of work, inmates generated over 15 million marks for SS coffers. Clearly, slave labor was big business for the Nazis.

Immediately after leaving quarantine, the women were subjected to the twice-daily routine of the *Appell*. Sirens awakened the inmates at four o'clock each morning. Prisoners had only a few short minutes to put on whatever warm clothing they had, crowd into the washroom, and march out to the large open square behind the administration building. Inmates were expected to array themselves in rows of five across to facilitate counting, but even so the process rarely took less than two hours. Often it was much longer before the SS could assure themselves that they had accounted for every prisoner, especially when there had been more than the usual number of deaths in the barracks the night before. Sometimes the SS guards seemed simply unable to add correctly, to the chagrin of the inmates forced to remain at attention for hours in all kinds of weather. In winter, frostbite occurred commonly, often leading in short order to gangrene, amputation, and death. Those suffering from dysentery were permitted no bathroom breaks; forced instead to simply relieve themselves where they stood. Prisoners too weak to continue standing were left on the ground where they fell, their fellow inmates forbidden to break ranks and offer assistance, lest the all-important count have to begin all over again. In the evening, when the exhausted inmates returned from their daily twelve-hour work shifts, the entire process took place all over again.

Before receiving their permanent work assignments, most of the prisoners, my grandmother most likely included, spent time as members of the *Verfügbaren*. This group inherited the most arduous job assignments, often involving excavating and road building, all without the benefit of machinery and always completely exposed to the elements. Some of the Verfügbaren were assigned to a special unit (*Sonderkommando*), a group of inmates charged with collecting the bodies of those who had died each night and carrying them to the crematorium. Being a member of the *Verfügbaren* was backbreaking work regardless of the task, but in spite of constant physical pain, hands covered with blisters, and a variety of other ailments, the SS permitted their prisoners no respite. Guards with attack dogs remained at the ready, waiting to pounce on any inmate who faltered.

VIII. RAVENSBRÜCK

*"Appell grounds with ruins of shower building in foreground
(Note crematorium with smokestack at rear)"*

The combination of daily hard labor and suddenly poor nutrition produced rapid weight loss. Many of the *Verfügbaren* shed as much as fifty pounds or more in their first two or three months in camp. The work had to go on, however. Regardless of the hardships, no prisoner wanted to appear unfit for work. The women were all well aware that those whom the Nazis regarded as a burden disappeared quickly.

Had Selma remained at hard labor in the main camp, she almost certainly would not have survived. Luckily, she found an alternative. By 1942, so many German men were serving in the Army that the civilian economy was struggling to supply sufficient goods to maintain the Nazi war effort. It didn't take long for the regime to figure out how to close the gap. The practice of renting the labor of concentration camp inmates had already been taking place for some time. It was only another short step for Hitler's men to convince German manufacturers to set up their factories in the camps themselves, where an endless supply of forced laborers would be readily available.

131

At the time, Siemens and Halske AG (the major German industrial conglomerate in business to this day) was the second largest producer of electrical components in the country. To protect the firm's position, company managers had cultivated relations with Heinrich Himmler, Hitler's most trusted lieutenant, whose brief also happened to include oversight of operations at Ravensbrück. Now, in response to Himmler's request, Siemens quickly agreed to construct two factories immediately adjacent to the walls of the camp. In late summer of 1942, manufacturing operations commenced with the assembly of parts for military telephones and submarine communications.

Scuttlebutt among the prisoners had it that life in the Siemens Camp was much better than in Ravensbrück proper. Many former inmates regard this conventional wisdom as nothing more than propaganda, but at a minimum, work in the centrally heated Siemens plants (to protect the sensitive electronics, not the prisoners) did offer a respite from hard labor exposed to the elements. As a result, the women of Ravensbrück competed fiercely for the Siemens jobs, and my grandmother was no exception.

Company managers insisted that prisoners be in reasonably good health, and that they pass certain tests of manual dexterity and general intelligence. This was a problem for Selma. Her intelligence was not at issue, but because of her chronically poor eyesight, she had always had difficulty with any kind of fine work. Despite these limitations, she managed to convince Siemen's testers that she could do the job, and by the fall of 1944 Selma had wangled a transfer out of the main camp to work in the company's factories.

Each morning after the *Appell*, the Siemens contingent exited through the front gates of Ravensbrück and squeezed themselves along a narrow one kilometer path between the quiet waters of the Schwedt Lake on one side and pens full of snarling SS dogs on the other. Their route to the Siemens *Lager* also took them past Ravensbrück's pigpens, and sometimes, on the way back at night, a few of the starving prisoners would sneak aside under cover of darkness to steal a bit of the slop meant for the hogs to eat.

The initial contingent of eighty Siemens laborers grew quickly as construction continued on additional factories. Crews of Ravensbrück inmates built thirteen new barracks to house the Siemens workforce and surrounded the entire installation with an electrified, double barbed-wire fence, creating a separate, self-contained compound immediately outside the walls of the main camp. Machine gun-toting guards patrolled from the watchtowers that stood at each corner of the enclosure. At its height in late 1944, the Siemens Camp consisted of some twenty factories, utilizing the forced labor of nearly 3,000 prisoners.

*"Area of former Siemens camp
(note remains of electrified barbed-wire fence at left)"*

Company employees ran the gamut from staunch Nazi ideologues to those genuinely concerned about the plight of the inmates. Because of the close interaction between prisoners and civilians, the SS insisted that all Siemens workers receive training in "proper" disciplinary methods. Those who were sympathetic had to be careful, as anyone caught taking too great an interest in the well-being of the prisoners could quickly find themselves out of a job. In general, the rules were more relaxed within the Siemens area, but the inability to work was not tolerated for any reason, physical abuse remained common, and the women were still treated more like goods than like people.

Any prisoner who was not productive enough or who faltered on the assembly line was beaten from behind with a rubber club by SS minders. The harsh conditions were all part of the Nazis' infamous strategy of *Vernichtung durch Arbeit* ("Extermination through Work"). Inmates whose performance did not improve found themselves transferred back to the main camp, usually reassigned to the *Verfügbaren*. Prisoners who were too weak or too sick to be useful were also sent back to the main camp, replaced by newer and younger workers selected by Siemens. After all, the company wasn't paying the Nazis good money for people who couldn't do the job.

By the time the Siemens factories first opened, rations in the main camp had dwindled to the point that hallucinations of food consumed the prisoners' minds. Eventually, company managers complained to their Nazi partners that the prisoners' starvation was affecting productivity, after which the food supply in the Siemens camp improved slightly, at least for a while. With Siemens paying the Gestapo nearly 5,000 marks per day for prisoner labor—funds that were critical for maintaining operations in the main camp—the company felt it should have some say over the treatment of its workforce.

The use of slave labor was always a double-edged sword for firms that collaborated with the regime. On the one hand, Siemens and others benefited from low production costs, easy discipline, flexibility in making work assignments and absence of the usual security problems. The downside, however, included poor productivity, a dearth of skilled labor, the constant need to train new workers due to the high attrition rate and the ever-present threat of sabotage.

Sabotage was the only way that workers could strike back at their masters, and in practice it took many forms, both inside and outside the Siemens facilities. Occasionally, groups of prisoners would simply refuse to perform certain types of work, especially tasks that supported the German war effort or directly harmed fellow prisoners. The most notable example of this were the repeated work slowdowns that occurred when camp administrators tried to use prisoner labor to build an improved gas chamber in early 1945. But since the Nazis always punished open defiance severely, such acts were rare.

Clandestine attempts were much more common, although these too had to be done carefully. Discovery was punishable by death, either quickly in front of the firing squad, or slowly and painfully by starvation in the Punishment Block. As with so many other aspects of concentration camp life, it was essential to know just how and when to flout the rules to minimize the chances of being caught. One group of Russian prisoners devised the particularly ingenious technique of rubbing garlic (a substance that was difficult for the Nazis to detect) on sensitive electrical contacts. In so doing they were able to render the equipment worthless for use later in the field.

Prisoners also built intentionally defective parts or knowingly passed substandard goods through the inspection process. Another favorite strategy was to falsify production records in order to conceal work slowdowns. When Selma first arrived in the Siemens camp, her fellow laborers quickly introduced her to the culture of sabotage at Ravensbrück. Even her "overseer," herself a half-Jew who had probably managed to avoid deportation by volunteering to serve, took my grandmother aside for a little talk. The *Aufseherin* whispered to Selma that things might go better for her if her work in the factory was "not too perfect."

As powerless as the prisoners were to affect the grim reality of their existence, seizing this small measure of control over something so important to their captors could be critical in motivating the prisoners to go on. Eventually, the problem became so widespread that the Nazi overseers became obsessed with rooting it out, tending to see sabotage everywhere, even when none had taken place. Not infrequently, guards meted out severe punishments to those who were in fact completely innocent.

In spite of frequent interruptions due to air raids, power outages, and repeated shortages of raw materials, work in the Siemens factories continued well into the spring of 1945. Finally, in the face of advancing Russian troops, officials closed down production and packed up all finished goods on hand for shipment. On April 29, the remaining Siemens workforce was transferred back to the main camp.

For a long time, all we had was my mother's recollection of what her own mother had told her about working for Siemens while in the camp. It turned out to be my brother, not long after we all returned from Ravensbrück, who found the definitive evidence corroborating Selma's story. He was poking around the online archives of the US Holocaust Museum in Washington one day and came across a listing for Nazi work records. A short time later, my mother and I went there to examine the reels of microfilm in detail. For hours, we read through page after page of handwritten records without finding a thing. I began to worry that, having scanned so many pages of often difficult-to-decipher gothic script, we had perhaps missed something important. We were just debating whether it would be better to wrap up for the day and come back fresh again the next morning when I found it. There, on the second-to-last page of the very last reel in the collection was an attendance record for one of the Siemens plants from mid-November 1944. Among the column of names along the left hand margin was written "Selma Zins." To the right, in columns representing each day of the week, were checkmarks indicating each day that my grandmother had toiled for the company on their concentration camp assembly line.

It was a stunning moment. At the time, I was still relatively early in my research, and up to that point, it had sometimes seemed like all the stories I had heard through the years had been only that — just stories. Though I never had reason to disbelieve any of it, here I was, staring at the incontrovertible proof of the slave labor that my grandmother had endured with the full complicity of Siemens' upper management, day after interminable day, all for the benefit of her Nazi captors and the company's bottom line.

Armed with this information, I decided to write to the public relations department at Siemens, asking if the company itself might have more detailed internal records about the work that my grandmother had done for them. Very quickly — much too quickly it seemed to me — I received back by overnight airmail from Germany a rather thick book detailing the company's history through the decades of its existence. Inside this weighty tome was a single chapter dealing with Siemens' role in the Nazi labor schemes, a couple of pages of which dealt specifically with the operation at Ravensbrück. No mention at all was made of individual prisoners. The polite letter tucked inside the package claimed that Siemens had not kept records regarding the names of specific inmates from this period. The response was so rapid, however, and the overnight shipment of such a heavy book seemingly so unnecessary, that I couldn't help thinking of Shakespeare's famous line in *Hamlet* — "The lady doth protest too much, methinks."

In the immediate postwar period, Allied tribunals caught and punished many of the overseers who had worked in the Siemens camp, but for years, the company itself resisted calls to compensate the prisoners whose unwilling efforts it had benefited from. It was not until the early 1960s that Siemens finally agreed to pay reparations to some 6,000 former inmates, mostly women from eastern bloc countries who had been involved in the firm's various concentration camp endeavors. Even then, Siemens' executives insisted on a very restrictive definition of who would qualify, and in no case did any single victim receive more than 3,300 German marks (the equivalent of less than $1,000 at the time). More recently, the company consented to take part in the comprehensive settlement brokered by the current German government in response to litigation begun in US civil courts. No doubt, the bean counters at Siemens saw this as a way to put a cap on the company's potential liability. By this time of course, the payments were far too late for most of the victims who, like my grandmother, had long since passed away. To this day, Siemens has yet to be held fully accountable for the profits it enjoyed from its partnership with Hitler's regime, and the company still refuses to divulge what it knows about individual slave laborers. I believe that Siemens should do the right thing at last by making public all of its internal records from the Nazi period and coming forward with additional damage payments to any of its living victims, whose remaining years might be made more comfortable by a share of the illicit profits that their own forced labor helped produce.

By the early spring of 1945, it was becoming clear to both guards and inmates alike in Ravensbrück that the war was rapidly coming to an end. Reliable information had always been hard to come by within the confines of the camp, but between the idle chatter with the civilian workers during the day and information passed on in the barracks by the new arrivals pouring in from the east at night, the women of Ravensbrück were able to get some sense of what was happening in the outside world. All through the month of April, the prisoners could also hear the sound of artillery fire off in the distance, as Red Army troops from the 49th Army of the 2nd Byelorussian Front advanced steadily on German positions.

Acknowledging that the end was near, Nazi officials began to evacuate the camp. On April 27 and 28, acting on the direct orders of Heinrich Himmler, guards at Ravensbrück assembled all those who appeared well enough to walk, including my grandmother, in groups of several hundred each. Even those women still able to move under their own power were nevertheless severely debilitated by that point. Most had had no soup for at least three days, no bread for ten, and no potatoes for more than half a year. Many of the would-be marchers wore civilian clothing, though always with the large white "X" marking them as inmates still visible on their backs. Before leaving camp, each prisoner received a Red Cross packet containing a blanket and a small ration of bread. Between fifteen and twenty thousand prisoners from Ravensbrück took part in what later became known as the *Todesmarsch* ("Death March"). Another two to three thousand women and children, too weak and sickly to move on their own, were left behind to fend for themselves, without food, water or electricity.

The reasons for the *Todesmarsch* remain obscure. Some historians have suggested that the Gestapo wanted to preserve a slave labor force to work in the munitions factories they still controlled farther to the west. More likely, I think, the regime hoped to use the prisoners as a bargaining chip when the inevitable moment of defeat came. It's also possible, given Nazi ideology, that Himmler was simply being vindictive. Even after years of investigation by scholars, however, no one really knows for sure just what Hitler's trusted lieutenants were hoping to accomplish.

As each group of marchers assembled, Nazi guards with dogs at the ready drove the women out through the front gates of the camp. Arrayed as always in rows of five, the prisoners strode back into the world they had left behind months or years before. For many of the inmates, the sights around them were things they had come to believe they might never experience again. But even though they had survived long enough to leave the concrete and barbed wire walls of the camp behind, the women of Ravensbrück were not yet completely free.

~:~

After I had finished wandering around Ravensbrück on that cold March day of our visit, I went to look for my mother. I was worried about how she was doing. Without discussing it beforehand, we had all scattered after passing through the camp gates that morning, each of us apparently wanting to be alone with his or her thoughts. Before our arrival, I had been a little concerned about how my mother might react to the visit. She was, after all, the only one among us to have actually known the family members who the Nazis had killed. There was bound to be, I thought, a huge difference between just hearing about what had happened to those you loved and actually seeing it for yourself.

After searching for a few minutes I found her standing alone, in front of the wall of flowers that serves as a memorial to all those who suffered and died at Ravensbrück more than half a century ago. Her eyes were a little red, but her mood was, if anything, defiant.

"You know what this means," she said to me, more of a statement than a question.

"I'm not really sure what you're getting at," I replied.

"Standing here now, with all of you, free to come and go as we please?" She paused for a moment.

"It means," she said, "that the Nazis didn't win."

"Author (center) with mother, siblings and cousin at Ravensbrück"

IX. LIFE GOES ON

After the Nazis took my grandmother away, Friedel and his two young daughters did their best to adapt to her sudden absence. Not only had Erika and Inge lost their mother, they had to adjust to the disappearance of many of their friends too. More and more, parents who could sent their children to live with relatives outside the city, where food was more plentiful and the threat of bombings much reduced. With so many students missing, not to mention the accumulating physical damage to the buildings themselves, local schools had long since stopped holding regular classes. Often, there was little for my mother and her sister to do. My grandfather, lacking anyone he trusted enough, kept Erika and Inge close by. Even if he had had someone to send his daughters to, Friedel couldn't bear the idea of having the girls separated from his watchful eye.

As the weeks and months passed by, the daily struggle for survival came to dominate the lives of everyone in the neighborhood. Erika and Inge spent much of their free time in the never-ending search for food. Productive capacity in the German economy had declined steadily as the war ground on, and in response the government repeatedly ratcheted down civilian rations. Worse yet, even those few essentials that the family was still entitled to had become impossible to find. During the day, while their father slept between work shifts, my mother and her sister joined the endless lines that snaked their way toward any shop that had something left to sell. Often they waited for many hours, only to find that by the time they got to the front, all the food was already gone. The two youngsters would trudge home to report to their father, all them facing yet another night of going to bed hungry. The warmer months, when the family could grow a bit of its own food, brought an occasional reprieve. Sometimes, when my grandfather had nothing left to put on the table, he gave each of his daughters a piece of black bread and sent them out into the garden to climb up into the family's plum trees and pick their own dinner of ripened fruit.

"Friedel and his girls — around the time of Selma's imprisonment"

From the time that Selma had first entered the hospital, Friedel's mother Maria had become a regular visitor to the family's apartment, trying to relieve her son of some of his daily burden. Although it was helpful to have a second adult around, Erika frequently clashed with her hard-to-please grandmother. As the older of the two sisters, she felt a growing responsibility to make up for her mother's absence. Standing in her way was *Oma* Maria. Just as she had tried to do earlier with Selma, Maria appointed herself the arbiter of everything her budding teenage granddaughter tried to accomplish. Knowing that the old woman's wrath could be fierce when she was dissatisfied, Erika held her breath each day while Maria ran her finger along the furniture to check for dust and inspected the corners of each room for specks of dirt she might have missed.

A few weeks after Selma was taken, Maria fell mortally ill. The diagnosis was cancer, and given the state of medical care in wartime Germany, death came quickly. The loss of her grandmother left Erika with jumbled emotions and more than a twinge of guilt. She had loved her *Oma* dearly, but the relief she felt at no longer having to face her harshest critic was undeniable.

With Maria no longer around to lend a hand, several of my grandfather's friends and acquaintances pitched in to help. I find this interesting for what it says about the willingness of some ordinary Germans, even at the height of Nazi power and influence, to come to the aid of "enemies of the regime" that they regarded as friends. One of the neighbors taught Erika how to iron a shirt for the first time. Another, Frau Schäfer, took Inge walking in the woods and taught her how to pick edible mushrooms to supplement the family's meager diet. When it happened that, not long after Selma had been deported, Erika experienced her first menstrual period, my grandfather asked the woman who coached the local handball team with him to teach his daughter what she needed to know. It turned out to be a fortuitous choice, as friend and daughter hit it off immediately, and Friedel's colleague became a surrogate mother of sorts for Erika. Sometimes when she felt especially troubled, my mother would spend the night at her new confidant's apartment, grateful for the chance to talk about whatever might be on her mind. I'm sure my grandfather was uncomfortable at first, dealing with some of the things his wife used to take care of, especially certain issues unique to adolescent girls. Once he realized there was no one else to turn to, however, he didn't shy from the task. Even when he couldn't handle things himself, he still found a way to meet the unique needs of his two young girls. Life hadn't stopped just because there was a war on.

From time to time in the early months after Selma's deportation,

Friedel and the girls would receive short notes from her in the mail. Occasionally a letter would trickle in from Jenny or Bertha in Theresienstadt as well. The Nazis heavily censored these messages from the camps, and prisoners were forbidden to divulge details about their living conditions, but at least the family knew where their loved ones were. Tempering their hopes that the writers were still alive, however, was the fact that they could never be sure how long it had been since the words they were reading had been written.

Even from the edited comments in the letters, it was obvious that food and warm clothing were in critically short supply in the camps, but there was frustratingly little that my grandfather and the girls could do to help. Whenever possible, Friedel would ship a package of food and clothing to Selma in Ravensbrück, though he had no way of knowing whether these precious items, squeezed from their own limited wartime supplies, ever reached their intended recipient. Gradually, the cards and letters stopped coming, and after several months, all communication with Selma and the rest of her Jewish relatives was lost.

Though Friedel and the girls worried constantly about what was happening to their loved ones, their own day-to-day battle for survival provided a strange respite of sorts. Compounding the family's concern for Selma was the ever-present fear that the Gestapo would come for one of them next. My grandfather lectured his daughters regularly about how important it was for them not to talk about their mixed heritage with anyone. He was adamant about this, but there was little need to remind Erika and Inge how painful the consequences of violating this critical rule could be.

My grandfather moved from job to job to keep the family afloat financially. His quest to Berlin had attracted unwanted attention from the Gestapo, who now seemed bent on punishing him for his audacity. Each time Friedel took a new position, local officials pressured his employers to keep him on piecework. Whenever he got proficient enough at a task to make a little more money, his superiors shifted him to another machine and forced him to start all over again. For a short time, in May 1944, Friedel worked as a machine punch operator for Alfred Tewes GmbH (a firm still in operation today), before moving on to the now-defunct Frankfurter Maschinenbau AG, where he managed to hang on until the end of the war. Unfortunately, the Gestapo did not limit themselves to on-the-job harassment. For months, officials kept trying to convince Friedel to divorce his Jewish wife while she was away, but this he steadfastly refused to do.

Inevitably, living under such a constant high level of stress took its toll. Not infrequently, Friedel had to miss work for medical reasons, most often due to a flare-up of the stomach ulcers that plagued him through-out his life. The family could ill afford these repeated absences, since when my grandfather was unable to work his only income consisted of short-term disability payments that were far less than his usual pay. Friedel hated being sick, but his health problems would later prove to be fortuitous, enabling him to hold off the Gestapo when, right before the end of the war, they decided to try to deport him, too.

At some point during Selma's absence (my mother can't be sure now exactly when it started), Friedel began an affair with Hanni Hansen, a woman who lived in an apartment upstairs in the same building. Frau Hansen's husband was an officer in the German army and had been away at the front for some time. Because of her husband's rank, my grand-father's mistress enjoyed a relatively privileged existence, with access to food and material goods not available to most of her neighbors.

At the beginning, noting how much her father seemed to care for this woman, Erika grew to like Frau Hansen as well, though later events would dispel this initial fondness. Unbeknownst to Friedel, his new mistress had carried on several other liaisons, some of them perhaps simultaneously. And although my grandfather was certainly a willing participant, he was no match for the determined and manipulative Frau Hansen. Hanni Hansen was used to getting what she wanted, and Frie-del, with his strongly developed sense of personal loyalty, made for an easy target. Even after the war was over and my grandparents had left for America, she tried to lure him back by claiming to be pregnant with their child. Friedel seriously considered returning, until one of his sisters-in-law reported seeing Frau Hansen's stained menstrual garments hanging on the clothesline between their apartments. Undeterred, my grandfather's former mistress continued to use her charms on the victorious American soldiers controlling her city, in yet another attempt to garner the increased rations and other privileges she had grown used to.

What particular advantage Hanni Hansen saw in spending her nights with a common laborer like Friedel Zins is unclear. Perhaps it was nothing more than a purely physical attraction to a handsome man who was, at least temporarily, without a partner. Though her later actions made it clear just how self-centered she was, my grandfather certainly could not see that at the time, and he grew quite close to his newfound lover. No doubt, he and Frau Hansen provided some measure of comfort to each other as each of them struggled to endure the harsh realities of life in wartime Frankfurt.

To this day, neither my mother nor Inge will criticize their father for his dalliance, and, in an important way, my grandfather's single greatest weakness only increases my own admiration for him. Despite his heroics, Friedrich Zins was no mythic, untouchable figure. He was a gentle and ordinary man, always warm and approachable. As a child I never had cause to fear him. His affair with Frau Hansen exposed in Friedel Zins the flaws and weaknesses we all share, and yet he was capable of unconquerable courage when faced with great challenges. Heroes, it seems to me then, can sometimes come in quite plain packages.

In Frankfurt, throughout the latter part of 1944 and into early 1945, Allied bombings intensified as the tide of the war began to shift. For Erika and Inge, the most frightening aspect of these attacks were not the explosions themselves, but rather the strafing runs that Americans and British planes had begun making in civilian areas. Despite the fact that pilots were under explicit orders in those last few months to take whatever measures necessary to force Germany to capitulate quickly, it's hard now to see the justification for these attacks. My mother can still recall clearly the visceral fear that erupted when she was caught outside when the fighters suddenly swooped in, streaking the ground with their deadly lines of fire. In less threatening times, my mother and her sister had spent hours playing with their friends in the open fields that lay just to the north of the family's apartment. In those last few weeks of the war however, it had become dangerous just to walk down the sidewalk, much less to stray over such unprotected ground. Friedel forbid his daughters to go anywhere near the open area, or even to play outside at all.

By late March 1945, more than a third of Frankfurt's prewar population had fled, but more than a quarter million people remained to endure the bombings. Over the course of three nights near the end of that month, the Allies dropped nearly 4,000 bombs throughout the city. By the time the assault was over, more than half of Frankfurt's 177,000 homes and apartments were uninhabitable. Lines for food, already hours long, became interminable. Paper money ceased to have any value. Survivors, more desperate than ever for warmth and shelter, took to scavenging through the bombed-out buildings, looking for wood, coal, or anything else that they could burn.

The air raids came so frequently at the end that the entire experience of being bombed came to seem almost routine. Often the Americans would attack during the day and the British again that same night, or vice versa. My mother's family had very mixed feelings about these Allied assaults. They feared for their own safety, of course, but deep down they also knew that the bombings were necessary if the war was ever going to end and there was any hope that their lives would get back to normal. Certainly they understood that if Hitler were to prevail, they would all be doomed. Even with the regime's tight control of information, most ordinary Germans had figured out that it was only a matter of time before the Nazis were defeated. Because of that, my grandfather and the girls almost looked forward to the Allied assaults, at least until the bombs started dropping and they had to run for their lives again. Towards the end, my mother and her sister wound up going to the bunker less and less often. With the raids coming so close together, often there just wasn't enough time to get there, and, as they had done at the beginning of the war, Erika and Inge resorted to taking what shelter they could in the reinforced cellar beneath their apartment.

By early 1945, Hitler's lieutenants abandoned all pretense of restraint against anyone with a Jewish connection. On January 18, local officials in Frankfurt published a list of some eighty men they planned to deport to the labor camp at Derenburg in the Harz Mountains of central Germany. Most of these were husbands of Jews the regime had deported previously — Aryans who had heretofore been left alone. The men received orders to appear at the main train station in three days' time. Though my grandfather's name did not appear on this first list, the real danger for him was just beginning.

On February 14, Nazi officials in Frankfurt decided to ship all remaining Jewish spouses from mixed marriages and their children, 159 adults and thirty-two children, to the concentration camps. These latest deportees boarded trains at the *Ostbahnhof* bound for Theresienstadt, just like the many thousands who had gone before them. Erika and Inge were not included on the list, and once again, my mother's family was somehow spared. In spite of the temporary reprieve, however, it was obvious to my grandfather that time was running out for all of them.

Friedel realized that he had to do something to try to get the girls to safety. He probably thought about asking his siblings for help, but even if one of them had been willing to take the risk, just sending his daughters to the other side of the city would not be enough. In his desperation to evade the authorities, he turned to Hans Fröhlich, his long-time family doctor. Dr. Fröhlich and his wife had been practicing in Praunheim since 1931. The couple's office stood at Am Ebelfeld 172, on a corner near the air raid bunker, not far from my grandparents' apartment.

Dr. Fröhlich was much beloved by the locals, especially for his habit of appearing without being summoned at the homes of those in need, having heard through the grapevine that one of his charges was ill.

More importantly, at least to my grandfather, Hans Fröhlich hated the Nazis. Though not Jewish himself, Dr. Fröhlich ignored the personal risk and used his position to protect as many of his patients from the regime as he could. Most often, this took the form of a trumped up medical excuse for a patient who was slated to be on the next transport out of the city. The doctor also gave freely from his own pocket to help Jews who had been barred from working and could no longer feed or support themselves. Dr. Fröhlich, as it turned out, wasn't the only one trying to help. Several other physicians in Frankfurt were of similar mind, and there may even have been a loose association of sorts among these kindred spirits. The Gestapo, though they must have been well aware of what was going on, chose not to confront the rogue doctors.

At Friedel's request, Dr. Fröhlich arranged for Erika to go to the *Elisabethhaus*, a children's home run by Protestant nuns in nearby Bad Nauheim. Officially, my mother was being sent there for treatment of a heart murmur, a condition that doctors had deemed worrisome enough at one point to require restricting her from sports activities at school. In reality, the condition was not all that serious, but it was a convenient excuse, enabling my grandfather, with the help of his doctor, to find a safer place for at least one of his children. No doubt the fact that Erika had been sent to Bad Nauheim before made it easier to justify this latest visit in the eyes of the authorities. Inge had been there once too, but this time she couldn't go — either because the home was either already filled with internal refugees or because Dr. Fröhlich couldn't fabricate a plausible enough reason to send her. Treatment at the *Elisabethhaus* consisted of enforced rest and improved nutrition, along with a regimen of spa sessions and salt baths. More importantly, the home was located outside the Allies' usual target area. Erika would now be farther from the prying eyes of the Gestapo and relatively safe from the bombings as well.

My mother arrived in Bad Nauheim to find children from a variety of backgrounds living at the home, many of whom had also been sent there under some pretense or other to escape the Allied attacks. Since it was impossible to be sure whom she could trust, it was imperative that Erika not divulge her Jewish connections to anyone. Of necessity then, she became something of a loner in spite of the *Elisabethhaus'* crowded confines. The need for caution was never clearer to my mother than on one day in mid-April when the children all huddled around the radio to hear German radio announcers gloat over the unexpected death of the American President, Franklin Roosevelt. Far from sharing in the jubilation of her peers, my mother worried about what would happen next, now that the man she regarded as her most powerful ally was gone.

On March 20, the Gestapo ordered a second group of men to report for transport to Derenburg, and this time there was no escape for Friedrich Zins. Frantic at the thought of having to leave his daughters behind, my grandfather once again turned to Dr. Fröhlich, the only person he could still trust. Friedel had seen the doctor frequently in the preceding few months, as the stress of the war years had taken its toll on his ulcers. Now his illness provided the perfect pretext, and all he had to do was ask. Hans Fröhlich was willing to do whatever he could to help. Friedel left the office with a two week stay on medical grounds, probably the most the two of them thought they could get away with. Once again, the Gestapo chose not to question the doctor's orders.

My grandfather had often told his daughters that if the Nazis ever came to take him away, he would shoot them both himself rather than leave them behind to face Hitler's men alone. My mother has her doubts about whether he would have actually followed through, and I too don't believe that Friedel could have ever harmed his own daughters, but none of us knows for sure. The pressures of war had led others to commit acts thought inconceivable in more normal times, and there *was* a gun in the house. Several months before, Erika had almost been killed when her father accidentally discharged the pistol while clean-ing it. That bullet had whizzed past my mother's head, into the back of the upholstered chair she was sitting in, and completely through the wall behind her out into the backyard. After the initial shock, Friedel's biggest worry had been that one of the neighbors might have heard the shot and would summon the police, but no one ever came to the door. Later, he went outside to search for the bullet, but was unable to find it.

All through the early spring of 1945, my grandfather ran his own private race against time. Acutely aware that the Nazis were closing in on the three of them, he also knew that American troops were advanc-ing closer to Frankfurt every day. By the middle of March, on the out-skirts of the city in Bad Nauheim, Erika and the other children could already hear the sounds of artillery fire in the distance. On March 29, 1945, only five short days before his medical reprieve would have ended, the US Army entered Frankfurt and seized control of the city. For Frie-del at least, the war was over.

Two weeks later, after he was certain that the fighting and the bomb-ings had ended, Friedel went to retrieve his daughter. The need for circumspection had passed, and my mother can still see the look of amazement on the face of Elisabeth Günther, the Mother Superior, when my grandfather finally disclosed the family's true heritage. It was not possible, Frau Günther had thought, for any child living under her close observation to have hidden such an important secret for so long.

X. FREEDOM

Of all the places I've gone in search of my grandparents' story, none has moved me more than my visit to the tiny village of Ifta, near the old east-west border in central Germany. It was there that my grandmother, with the aid of the town baker, an obscure little man with a fortunate penchant for part-time farming, at last got her chance to go home again.

Paula Kutscher, my grandparents' good friend and neighbor in Frankfurt, had grown up in Ifta, where her stepfather, Berthold Busch, operated his business out of the ground floor of the family home. Each morning, fellow villagers would come calling for their fresh bread at the heavy wooden half-door that guarded the entrance to the bakery. Christa Bauer, who is Herr Busch's granddaughter (and Paula's niece) still lives nearby, and one day in March 2001 my mother and Doris and I went to visit her at her modern-looking home at the edge of town. Over the years, I had heard the story of my grandmother's escape from the Eastern Zone many times — how the Busch family had taken Selma into their home and then plotted a way to smuggle her out of Soviet-controlled territory. In the half century or so since those dramatic events had taken place, my mother had forgotten some of the details. As it turned out, Christa Bauer had heard the story too — from her own grandfather when she herself was a child. As we sat and talked through the afternoon, she slowly filled in the missing pieces for us.

*"Christa Bauer (center), granddaughter of Berthold Busch,
with Erika and Doris in Ifta"*

My grandmother's final ordeal began back in the spring of 1945, while
she was still clinging to life inside Ravensbrück. Unbeknownst to Selma,
her own brother-in-law was fighting for the Nazis in the surrounding
region. Wilhelm Zins, Friedel's older brother, had been drafted into the
German Third Battalion, which was now engaged in a futile attempt
to resist the Soviet advance. Wilhelm died in battle just before the end
of the war, almost certainly without realizing that he had been trying
to keep the Russians from liberating the very camp where his brother's
wife was being held, not that he would have had much choice in the
matter even if he had known.

To my knowledge, my grandmother never talked to anyone about her
experiences immediately after leaving Ravensbrück. In trying to recon-
struct what had happened to her, I sought in vain to find a fellow survivor who had known Selma personally during her time in the camp.
That search eventually led me to the book by Katharina Katzenmeier,

the one I found so helpful in describing life inside Ravensbrück itself. In her book, Frau Katzenmeier also talked about taking part in the Death March, and of traveling for a time afterwards with another former inmate, Else Nüßler, a woman who my grandmother had also mentioned as one of her companions during this period. Later in my research, I came across an additional unpublished account by Katharina Katzenmeier that mentioned Selma Zins by name. From that and other stories of the final days of Ravensbrück, along with the few details that my mother can recall hearing when she was younger, I've tried to imagine what my grandmother's own experience during the *Todesmarsch* must have been like.

Selma's group exited the gates of Ravensbrück just one day before the Russian liberators arrived. The marchers' intended destination was the Nazi work camp at Malchow, some seventy-five kilometers distant. All through the day and night, the inmates moved forward without a break as the sounds of battle surrounded them. Not long after my grandmother's group left the camp, a large explosion occurred back in the direction they had come from. Red Army troops had destroyed a munitions bunker in the adjacent town of Fürstenberg. The impact stunned both guards and prisoners, and in the resulting confusion, a few of the women seized the opportunity to flee into the woods.

For the next ten days, guards drove the prisoners relentlessly to the north and west, through the town of Neustrelitz, across the German state of Mecklenburg, and towards Nazi-controlled strongholds near the Baltic Sea. Those in charge had made no provisions for food or shelter en route, so prisoners scavenged at the side of the road for whatever sustenance they could find. Sleep was permitted only for short periods, always in the open and without shelter during those cold nights in early spring. Dogs attacked any stragglers, who were sometimes shot in their tracks and left where they had fallen. Along the way, the former inmates encountered many other groups moving on foot — an eclectic jumble of retreating soldiers, refugees from eastern lands, and local inhabitants fleeing the Soviet Army advance. Despite their own deprivations during the long war, most of these displaced souls were in much better condition than the women of Ravensbrück.

As the bedraggled columns shuffled on, the prisoners took note of how beautiful much of the surrounding countryside remained. Blue skies framed well-kept houses, some of them still sporting bursts of colorful flowers in the windows, things that none of the inmates had seen for the years they had spent behind concentration camp walls. Strangely, even in those villages that seemed untouched by war, there were few people out and about, although animals often roamed freely in the streets. Occasionally, local inhabitants would offer the marchers food or water, but even at this late date the Nazi guards refused to let their prisoners accept any outside assistance.

As the Death March wore on, day after day, groups of marchers from Ravensbrück began to diverge and escapes became increasingly common. Prisoners often hid in the woods after dark, waiting for the rest of the inmates to move on without them. With the trees not yet leafed out enough in the early spring to provide reliable cover, this could be risky business. Russian women in particular felt compelled to break away from their captors, hoping to head back eastward in search of friendly troops from home. Many other prisoners also entertained thoughts of flight, but the harsh realities of their situation held them back. Women traveling alone with no food or water, often sick and still in prison dress, would be completely at the mercy of the other desperate souls now filling the roads. Thievery and rape were rampant, so much so that more than a few former prisoners even sought to rejoin the groups of marchers, once again submitting themselves to the Nazi guards rather than risk traveling the roads alone.

Before long, the SS officers themselves began to flee, leaving their subordinates behind to guard the prisoners. Some of those who remained attempted to exchange their uniforms for the prisoners' clothing, hoping to blend in with the innocent. A few were even brazen enough to try to befriend their former captives. Not surprisingly, survivors rebuffed these efforts. Over time, the distinction between guards and prisoners evaporated, and one morning, when Selma and the other prisoners awoke, their guards had simply disappeared. Confusion was immediate. After years of sharply regimented camp life, the former inmates suddenly faced the prospect of managing entirely on their own, in the midst of the most hostile surroundings imaginable. Dirty and starving, many could barely walk, more than a few were sick and feverish, and all were bereft of warm clothing. The situation demanded bold action, but the women were no longer used to making decisions for themselves. They soon realized that, despite their momentary freedom, they were stuck deep within the Russian-controlled zone. My grandmother's group elected to head west, searching for the most direct route to the American or British lines.

Over the next several nights, my grandmother and her companions occasionally found shelter in a barn or other abandoned structure, but mostly they slept out in the open, subsisting on the flesh of dead horses in the roadway and on unripe apples stolen under cover of darkness from the owners' trees. Sometimes, the desperate survivors approached residents of the towns they passed through, begging for food or a place to spend the night. Most of the locals reacted with fear and revulsion at the sight of the emaciated concentration camp survivors. Outright refusals were common, due at least in part to the lingering air of anti-Semitism in the country. A few did share what little they had left, but still the former inmates had to be careful. Eating too much good food too soon after so long a period of starvation could provoke a sometimes fatal intestinal reaction.

As the women journeyed on, the composition of the survivors' group fluctuated. Some survivors broke away to head in the direction of home, others would reappear out of nowhere to rejoin their former comrades. In general, the newly freed prisoners were accepting and supportive of their fellow former inmates, even those they did not know — an attitude borne of their shared suffering. The refugees reserved their suspicions mainly for German women, who were required to prove that they were not SS or Gestapo trying to conceal themselves amongst their former captives. In the confusion and chaos at the end of the war, few people had any official documents, and differentiating friend from foe was often impossible.

For the most part, the companions traveled on by foot, though occasionally they managed to hitch a ride for a short distance, crammed in with other refugees on the back of a jeep or farm truck. In spite of their poor physical condition, the former prisoners kept on moving, spurred by the taste of freedom and an overwhelming desire to see their homes and families again. The stronger and more determined in the group urged their weaker sisters to persevere. After having endured so much, no one wanted to see a friend succumb so soon before reaching home again.

Even when Selma and her companions were able to find food and shelter, danger remained close at hand. American and British warplanes, still hunting for retreating German Army units, continued to attack regularly, inadvertently catching refugees traveling on the open roads in the crossfire. Fighters could materialize without warning, strafing the ground with bullets and sending the former prisoners scampering for the protection of the nearest stand of trees. More than a few camp survivors lost their lives in these assaults. Closer to the ground there were additional hazards as well. Soviet soldiers, weary of war but eager to claim their spoils, had a well-earned reputation for preying upon defenseless refugees, especially Germans. Seemingly undeterred by the haggard condition of the women, soldiers would break into buildings where groups of travelers had sought safe haven, searching for easy targets to satisfy their lust.

Gradually, my grandmother's troupe turned southwards, heading in the general direction of Frankfurt and home. Without maps, however, the companions could never be sure exactly which direction they were going. Especially in the early days after their release, the small band had to be on the lookout for impromptu checkpoints, often set up by individual SS members who had taken it upon themselves to search the tide of refugees for former concentration camp inmates. Ironically, hitching a ride on a German army truck could sometimes be the former prisoners' best protection, since SS members usually allowed these vehicles to pass through without inspection. To lessen their risks, the women stayed off the main roads and restricted most of their movements to after dark, which slowed their progress significantly.

Prisoners who had been left behind at Ravensbrück fared better than their counterparts out wandering the roads. After the Russians took over the camp, soldiers quickly erected a field hospital to treat the sick inmates, though many were in such advanced states of debilitation that they died anyway. Within a few days, international relief organizations moved in and began to repatriate the survivors. For those still out in the countryside, beyond the reach of any official organization, help was a great deal harder to find.

Eventually, my grandmother's party dwindled down to just three: herself, Else Nüßler, and a woman she continued to refer to in the traditionally formal German way as Frau Heymann. As the travelers made their way back through the city of Leipzig, Selma fell ill, probably a result of having eaten contaminated horseflesh. She labored on, and by mid-August, the three women had reached Eisenach, a medium-sized city near the border of the Soviet-controlled zone. In the three months since leaving Ravensbrück, they had wandered over 500 kilometers together through eastern Germany, almost all of it on foot, with little or no outside assistance. Initially, Selma and her companions went unnoticed in the crush of refugees that had descended on the city, so, like many other new arrivals, the trio of friends spent their first couple of nights still sleeping out in the open.

Eisenach had been a hotbed of popular resistance to the Nazis, and after the war ended, it became a focal point for displaced persons returning to the West. A group of prominent women in the city had formed the

Antifaschistischer Frauenausschuss, an organization dedicated to assisting victims of Hitler's regime. With the tacit approval of the new Soviet military administration, these same altruistic souls were now helping the stream of refugees pouring in. One member of the group, Julie Schulz Erben, owned a local guesthouse called the *Hotel zur Tanne*, located in a three-story building at Barfüsserstrasse 4, near the southern edge of Eisenach. There, the *Frauenausschuss* had arranged to house a number of returnees from Theresienstadt, Auschwitz and other camps. Within a few days of their arrival, Selma and her two friends obtained a room at the *zur Tanne* as well. It was the first real shelter the women had enjoyed since leaving Ravensbrück back in the spring. (Sadly, decades later the *Hotel zur Tanne* had fallen into disrepair, its upper two floors essentially uninhabitable, and in late 2002 city officials demolished the building.)

"The Hotel zur Tanne, Eisenach (at right)"

The companions had not been in Eisenach for long before my grandmother's friends realized that her condition was deteriorating rapidly. On August 20, 1945, Frau Nüßler and Frau Heymann took Selma across town to the *Wartburg Klinikum*, where she was promptly admitted, critically ill, with what was later determined to be typhoid fever. She spent the next two and a half months under the care of Dr. Winter, one of the staff physicians. At the time, there were no antibiotics available to treat civilians, so care consisted of intravenous fluids and bowel rest. Under the prevailing medical wisdom of the day, the doctors did not begin to feed typhoid patients until their fever had completely resolved, presumably indicating that the intestines had healed sufficiently to safely permit the passage of food again. As her condition improved, however, Selma's hunger grew unbearable. Eventually, she became so desperate to eat that she shook down the mercury in her thermometer to make it appear as if her fever had disappeared — a misguided attempt to fool her nurses that resulted in a near-fatal relapse. In a last-ditch effort, Selma's doctors conducted an experimental plasma exchange to try to clear the bacterial toxins from her system. The procedure ultimately saved her life.

"The Wartburg-Klinikum in Eisenach circa 1945"

Until Selma entered the hospital in Eisenach, my grandfather had had no way of knowing where his wife was, or even that she had survived at all. After the war ended, Friedel had made repeated attempts to locate her, but none of the lists of liberated prisoners published by the Red Cross and other organizations included the name of Selma Zins. In Frankfurt, after returning from Theresienstadt himself, Rabbi Leopold Neuhaus set up the *Betreuungsstelle* to assist survivors in finding family members and reestablishing their lives. In June 1945, my grandfather and his neighbor Alex Boneberger went there together to search for their relatives, only to discover that the Jewish agency had no information about Selma either.

Despite the lack of news, Friedel and his daughters kept hoping that Selma was still alive somewhere. My grandfather began searching privately for other camp survivors who might be able to tell him something about his wife, but since there had never been a large Jewish population in Praunheim to begin with, the number of returnees in the immediate area was quite small. The few who did come back could offer him no information. Later that summer, Heinz Baer, a distant cousin of Selma's, returned home from Theresienstadt. When Friedel went to see him, Heinz told him how the Nazis had deported Jenny, Bertha, and the three children out of Theresienstadt a second time, but what had happened to them after that he did not know. About Selma, he had no information at all.

It was Else Nüßler, who had walked all that way to Eisenach with Selma, who first brought the news of her survival back to Frankfurt. She was quick to caution Friedel and the girls, however, that all was not well. She described how serious Selma's condition had been when the friends brought her to the hospital. Several more anxious weeks ensued. At last, a postcard from my grandmother herself appeared in the mail, announcing her recovery. The family soon found out, however, that there was still one large obstacle preventing Selma's long-delayed return home.

Laufende Nr.	Monat:							Zahl der			Vorname und Stand des Vaters
	Vor- und Zuname	Stand oder Gewerbe	Geburtsort	Wohnort	Geburts-Jahr und Tag	Religion	Geschwister	Kinder			
								unter	unmündig		
640		Hebamme	Poppenlauer	Dörrheim?	2.8.07	kath.					
641		Ehefrau	Wester-Zapzau	Eisenach	1.7.13	kath.					
642		Schüler	Stadtfeld	Stadtfeld	24.12.30	ev.					
643		Dr. med.	Berlin	Eisenach	23.3.09	ev.					
644	Zins, Selma	Ehefrau	Frankfurt/M.	Eisenach	3.10.07						Friedrich ...
645		Ehefrau	Kl. Dornbach	z.Zt. Eisenach	25.11.18	kath.					
646		Forstfahrer	Eisenach	Kreuzspring	5.3.14	ev.					
647		Ehefrau	Böttchen	Kreuzspring	1.11.21	kath.					
648		Ehefrau	Unterhaus	Eisenach	22.6.13	kath.					
649		Kind	Eisenach	z.Zt. Wölfa	16.7.45	ev.					
650		Kind	Eisenach	z.Zt. Eisenach	13.7.45	ev.					
651		Kind	Oberachsterhausen	Eisenach	2.3.45	ev.					
652		Kind	Eisenach	Eisenach	1.6.45	ev.					

"Wartburg-Klinikum register containing entry for Selma Zins"
and "pg. 2 of register (arrow denotes Selma's entry)"

2

Vor- und Geburtsname der Mutter	Wohnung I. des Vaters II. der Mutter	Vor- und Geburtsname des Mannes bezw. der Frau	Krankenkasse	Krankheit	Tag der Aufnahme	Entlassen als			Gestorben	Verpflegungstage			Bemerkungen
						geheilt	erleichtert	ungeheilt		I. Klasse	II. Klasse	III. Klasse	
	Poppenlauer, z.Zt. Dörrheim...	Selbstz.		Typhus-Verd.	18.8							3	Dr. Winter
	z.Zt. Eisenach, Ziehenloben...	Fern. Ordrmd.		Typholis	19.8							3	Dr. Winter
Hilda ?	Stadtfeld, Unterland 2	Selbstzahlen		Diphtherie	19.8							3	Dr. Winter
	z.Zt. Eisenach, Stadt. Schule	Wolff, Inst.		Diphtherie	19.8							3	Dr. Winter
→	Eisenach, Hotel Tanne 2			Typhus-Verd.	20.8	24.						3	Dr. Winter
	z.Zt. Eisenach, Theat. Schule	Wolff, Inst.		Diphtherie	20.8							3	Dr. Winter
	Kreuzspring, Schöne Aussicht	A.O.K. Eis.		Typhus-Verd.	20.8				28.9			3	Dr. Winter
	Kreuzspring, Schöne Aussicht	A.O.K. Eis.		Typhus-Verd.	30.8	9.10						3	Dr. Winter
	Eisenach, Zellerstr. 35	A.O.K.		Typhus-Verd.	30.8				6.10			3	Dr. Winter
Ottilie G.	Ohlau, z.Zt. Wölfa, Gotha	Barmen Ersatzk.		Ernährungsst.	30.8							K	Dr. Hackmack
Elisabeth	Berlin, z.Zt. Tannenburg	Selbstz.		Ernährungsst.	30.8							K	Dr. Hackmack
Use S.	Eisenach, Schönsmützenstr.	A.O.K. Eis.		Darmkatarrh	30.8.							K	Dr. Hackmack
Gisela S.	Eisenach, Trebonius str.	A.O.K. Eis.		Durchfall	31.8							K	Dr. Hackmack
Gertrud	Eisenach, Stadtfeldstr. 7A	A.O.K. Eis.		Darmkatarrh	30.8	14.9						K	Dr. Hackmack

Selma left the *Wartburg Klinikum* on November 2, 1945. In the months that she had been ill, the Soviet Army had consolidated its control over the Eastern Zone and was increasingly restricting passage over the border. By the end of 1945, the Russians were routinely refusing to permit refugees, even camp survivors with families in the West, to leave. Had she not gotten so ill and been able to return home sooner, or even if she had remained in camp and come under the auspices of the Red Cross, Selma's return home would have been far less complicated. As it was, having survived sixteen months in a Nazi concentration camp and a near-fatal bout of typhoid, my grandmother was once again trapped, unable to leave the Soviet Zone and return to her loved ones in Frankfurt.

Friedel was at a loss. One day, while talking about Selma's predicament with his friends Otto and Paula Kutscher, Paula told him that she was planning to go to the Eastern Zone herself. The village where she had grown up was now located behind the Russian lines, and she had heard very little from her parents since the end of the war. Paula wanted to go back home to see for herself that her mother and stepfather were okay. She had hesitated to make the trip up until then, uncertain whether the Soviets would allow her to return to the West. Now, she said, she had more than one reason to take the risk. Paula's hometown lay only a few kilometers north of Eisenach, where Selma remained trapped. She told Friedel she would go into the city, locate his wife, and try to find a way to get her safely across the border. My grandfather did not want to endanger his friend, but knew of no other way to get Selma back. Reluctantly, he agreed to Paula's plan.

Not long after arriving in the Soviet zone, Paula found Selma and brought her to the Busch family home in Ifta. Paula's parents occupied a small brick house at Am Markt 5, not far from the center of the village. Having never met a camp survivor before, Paula's parents must have been shocked at first by Selma's appearance, but they took her in

"Paula Busch Kutscher in 1942"

warmly just the same. Over the next several days, Paula and her step-father put together their plan for getting the two women home.

Herr Busch had no political contacts that might have helped, but the family did own some land north and west of the village that ran right up to the edge of the Russian Zone. Paula's father farmed this acreage to supplement his modest income. Later, the Soviets would confiscate the Busch family land to create a buffer zone around the border, but in late 1945 they were still permitting Berthold Busch to tend his own fields unescorted.

"Berthold Busch (undated prewar photo)"

Paula and her father had an idea. The family owned a *Mistwagen*, a horse-drawn cart they used primarily for spreading manure. Mounted across the front was a rectangular wooden box for the driver to sit on. At the rear, an open cargo bed sat atop the four iron-banded wheels.

Late one night, the two women squeezed themselves into the hollow box under the front seat. Had Selma not been so emaciated, they almost certainly would not have fit. Herr Busch climbed on top and spurred his horses forward. The urge to go quickly must have been irresistible, but to avoid attracting attention Herr Busch kept the cart moving at a leisurely pace as he approached the outskirts of the village.

"The Mistwagen"

166

Had the Soviets stopped and searched the wagon, the three of them would almost certainly have wound up in the gulag, or worse. After what seemed like a very long time, the *Mistwagen* finally crested the last hill before the border. Off to the left, up on a ridge, a line of evergreen trees offered some cover. The old man brought the horses to a halt, and the two women crawled stiffly out from beneath the wooden seat. Little was said as Paula hugged her stepfather tightly, neither of them knowing when or if they might ever see each other again. Then, she took Selma's hand and led her friend, still weak and unsteady on her feet, down off the high ground. Slowly, the two women made their way across the rolling hills towards the soft cluster of lights just visible in the distance. Four kilometers away, they reached the first village on the Western side. When morning came, they boarded a train for home.

"Edge of Busch family land today
(Note Soviet-era fence at right and tree-lined ridge in background)"

Ever since my visit to Ifta, I've thought a great deal about why Paula and her father would have put themselves at such great risk to help my grandmother, a woman to whom they owed nothing. From Christa

Bauer, Berthold Busch's granddaughter, I learned that the family had a tradition of helping those in need. During the war, Paula's parents had taken in wounded soldiers from both sides and nursed them back to health. Once, when they tried to help an injured Allied pilot, angry villagers had shot the man dead in the front hall of the family's home, but even that did not deter Herr Busch. Partly then, Paula was simply following the example her parents had set for her, but I believe that there is more to it than that.

In the decades since the Holocaust, the German people have received their fair share of blame, rightly so perhaps, for not protesting Nazi atrocities while they were occurring. Less noted however, is the substantial number of stories about ordinary Germans risking life and liberty to come to the aid of Jewish victims. Paula Kutscher and her parents were such people, and in their own small way, maybe without consciously realizing it, I think they sought to make amends for some of the crimes that the Nazis had committed in their name.

Standing on that rise outside Ifta sixty years later, looking out over the gentle hills at the villages in the distance, it was not hard to imagine what it must have been like the night my grandmother began her final journey towards home. In the months after Paula and Selma's escape, the Soviets confiscated the Busch family land and erected a twelve-foot-high fence across the parcel, marking the edge of the former Eastern bloc. When the Berlin Wall fell, the German government returned the farmland to Herr Busch's descendents. After much discussion, the townspeople of Ifta decided to leave the fence in place, as a reminder of what they have at long last regained.

At the end of my visit, Christa Bauer took me back to her grandparents' home in the village for one last look around. As we relaxed in the garden behind the house and talked, I glanced over her shoulder back at the house. There, leaning up against the wall to accent the yard, stood the four ancient wooden wheels that had carried my grandmother to freedom so many years ago.

X. FREEDOM

"The Wheels"

XI. AFTERMATH

Just after dawn on a crisp December morning, three sharp rings sounded at my grandparents' apartment in Frankfurt, announcing a visitor at the door. It was the family's pre-arranged signal — meant to indicate that it was safe to let in one of their own. Inside the tiny bedroom they shared, just off the front hallway, Erika and Inge sat up, rubbed the sleep from their eyes, and shot each other a quizzical glance. Who could *that* be?

They knew their father was "upstairs" — the code word the sisters used when their father spent the night with his mistress. Besides, he had his own key and could have let himself in. Cautiously, with the older girl in the lead, the two crept out of their room and felt their way along the hallway. Reaching the door, Erika knelt down and peered through the mail slot to see who was there, just as her father had taught her to do. The toothless, white-haired figure that filled her rectangular field of vision was almost unrecognizable.

"*Wer ist da?*" she asked, already knowing what the answer must be.

"*Mutti,*" came the soft reply.

Selma was home at last.

Erika unfastened the lock and eased open the door, still not entirely sure about the identity of this strange apparition. Tentatively, she stepped forward and put her arms around her mother's rail-thin waist. Behind them, Inge had glued herself to the wall. After a few moments, Erika released her embrace. Then she scrambled upstairs to get her father.

I don't know what my grandparents said to each other in those first

171

few moments after they were reunited, or if Selma realized right away just where her husband had been. Inevitably, those who returned home from Hitler's camps faced tremendous emotional and psychological hurdles attempting to readjust to normal life, and my grandmother would be no exception. This certainly wasn't going to make it any easier.

She wasn't the only one who had adjustments to make. After the initial rejoicing, Erika and her mother began to clash frequently. Having taken over most of the day-to-day running of the household while Selma was away, Erika had become accustomed to doing things without adult supervision. Now, as a teenager whose maturity had been accelerated by the necessities of life in time of war, she chafed at having her mother in charge once again.

Like so many others, Selma also had to cope with the realization that not a single member of her immediate family had come back alive: her parents, Jenny and Berthold, her sister Bertha, Bertha's husband, and their three children — all of them had been exterminated. Of my grandmother's entire extended family, only her distant cousin, Heinz Baer, and her stepfather's sister, Minna Stein, had survived.

While in the camps, Selma, like many other prisoners, had maintained her sanity by clinging to her former identity, but this only intensified the sense of disorientation she felt upon returning to find that everyone else was gone. Even for those who had personally witnessed the deaths of their loved ones, the reality of the loss was sometimes only completely understood after returning home again. With friends and relatives no longer present, the lives that returnees had known before the war had simply ceased to exist.

Selma frequently lapsed back into her camp mentality. She found it impossible to shed her constant obsession with food, and it would be a long time before my grandmother could bring herself to throw out anything even remotely edible, no matter how rotten or unappetizing it might seem. Erika once found her mother preparing soup for dinner out of some discarded potato peelings, even though fresh vegetables were no longer hard to find. More disturbing yet, Selma couldn't understand why her daughter objected to eating such unappetizing gruel.

After the hard life of the camp, my grandmother required ongoing medical care for a variety of lingering ailments, and treatment could be hard to find in the immediate postwar period. For a time, she attended the *Wiedergutmachungsstelle* ("making-well-again station"), a facility set up by city officials specifically to meet the unique needs of concentration camp survivors. Many of my grandmother's problems were purely physical, but she also experienced anxiety attacks and other vague but distressing symptoms. Eventually, her doctors sent her to an *Erholungsheim* — a specialized recuperative facility located some distance outside the city. In addition to the medical treatments, food was more plentiful there, which the doctors hoped would allow Selma to regain her strength more quickly. (In fact, after gorging for weeks on a diet overly rich in potatoes and other starches, she returned to Frankfurt having gained over 40 pounds and looking quite bloated.) But even after her time at the spa, my grandmother's anxiety attacks persisted. Today, we would diagnose her as having Post Traumatic Stress Disorder (a syndrome not recognized until after the Vietnam War). At the time, however, her symptoms continue to puzzle both Selma and her doctors.

Even if doctors had understood the cause of Selma's ailment, it might not have mattered much. The interim government in Frankfurt offered little in the way of mental health services, and the general public didn't have much empathy for the plight of concentration camp survivors either. In the weeks and months immediately after the war ended, most people were consumed with the daily tasks of just getting by, and few wanted to think about what had taken place in Hitler's death camps. Many of the city's residents, having endured years of Allied bombing attacks, were convinced that their own privations had been at least as bad as anyone else's, and there was a strong sense of just wanting to move on. Friends and neighbors expected returnees from the camps not to appear bitter or downcast, and they shunned those who displayed their grief too openly. Ironically, having returned to homes that no longer provided any comfort or solace, more than a few who survived the Nazis wound up taking their own lives.

Most found their own ways to cope. Not surprisingly, survivors often turned to each for counseling. Selma's aunt, Minna Stein, who had not only lost her husband, but her only son and his wife and their two children as well, later achieved some measure of notoriety for founding a support group for other Jewish women who had returned alone. My grandmother, for whatever reason, never sought her aunt's help, nor did she receive any other formal treatment that we know of. Instead, Selma battled her demons alone.

Restoring trust proved to be another major obstacle. Those who came back looked at others and wondered, "Is he sympathetic?" or "Would she have helped me when I was in need?" Every Jew also had to ask himself why he had returned when so many others had perished. This questioning provoked a need in returnees to accomplish something significant with the remainder of their days, as if to make up for all the lives the Nazis had cut short. Many survivors felt they had a duty to be happy, as if those who did not return expected no less of them. These were weighty burdens to shoulder, particularly for people who had been so recently and severely traumatized.

Most survivors longed to be like everybody else again, but those who had endured the life and death struggles in the camps often found it difficult to take seriously all the little things of day-to-day existence. Returnees also felt that having endured so much, they should not have to work so hard again so soon. With help scarce and the number in need so great, survivors had little choice but to find ways to support themselves, despite the fact that their earlier deportations had often interrupted promising careers or educational paths. The relentless demands of reintegrating led many to feel as if they were "living without being alive," in the words of one concentration camp veteran.

Lacking self-confidence after their long incarceration, many survivors had to re-learn normal social behaviors as well—to offer a polite smile instead of a grimace in response to signs of friendliness for instance. Everything that had previously been so familiar now seemed foreign. Most found it hard to shed their ingrained sense of vigilance, and constant feeling that another catastrophe was just around the corner. Returnees tried to accomplish this by imitating the way their "normal" friends and family members acted and thought. Some survivors described the feeling of watching themselves from the outside, as if what was occurring to them at that moment was actually happening to someone else.

Those who came back often had the sense that their new friends and acquaintances were painfully vain — seemingly obsessed with the trivial details of their lives and ignorant of the suffering the Jews had endured. Family members shied away from talking about what had happened in the camps, partly because of their own discomfort, but also in a misguided attempt to avoid upsetting those they cared about. When the subject did come up, conversation would be quickly redirected, even though most survivors did not want to let go of the memories of loved ones they had lost. Ordinary small talk became tiring. While friends were discussing their latest romances, survivors spent much of their time searching for their murdered relatives. Drained and warped by experiences that set them irreparably apart, returnees dared not talk about how strange and disconnected they felt.

Former prisoners sometimes returned home only to find that their partners, having long since assumed they were dead, had moved on with their lives. As with my grandparents, spouses had sometimes established new intimate relationships that made it almost impossible for survivors to fit back in. Marriages among survivors occurred frequently in the immediate postwar period, and these were unions that tended to last — the partners bound together by experiences that no one else could share. To be in the company of someone else who did not need explanations, who had been there and understood, was for many an indispensable anchor in those first few months and years.

My grandparents had their own issues to work out. As close as they might have been at one time, their wartime experiences had now made them two very different people, and they faced the difficult task of getting to know each other all over again. Complicating the situation was Friedel's unwillingness to break off his affair with Hanni Hansen.

My grandfather's relationship with his mistress was complex. While he certainly made his choices of his own free will, he was also in well over his head with the scheming Frau Hansen, whose own husband never returned from the front. No doubt Friedel was reluctant to give up the physical pleasures he had grown used to, but there was much more to it than that. The same fierce personal loyalty that had earlier led him to risk his freedom on the ill-fated trip to Berlin to save Selma now made it impossible for him to simply abandon someone he had grown to care so much about. It didn't take long for Selma to realize that the rift caused by Friedel's extramarital affair was not likely to resolve itself as long as the family remained in Frankfurt.

My grandmother needed a fresh start in a place where the memories might not haunt her as much, and more importantly, where she would never be at risk in the same way again. With her extended family all gone, there was nothing to hold her in Frankfurt, and there was never any question that my grandparents were going to leave Germany. Everyone Selma had left was in New York, not only Hermann and Rosi, but also most of Jenny's siblings and their growing families, with whom perhaps there would be a chance to reconnect.

My mother recalls even as a child having the strong sense that in America, her family could at last put the trauma of the war years behind them. Neither she nor Inge had any qualms about leaving behind everything that was familiar, and they were determined to put on a brave face for their parents.

I don't know whether my grandfather would have chosen to leave Germany if his wife had not come back, but I strongly suspect not. It was Friedel who had the most ambivalence about leaving, and although his original economic incentive for making the move still held, the case for my grandfather to take his daughters to a strange new country would have been much less compelling once the Nazi threat was past. Friedel was also a member of a large and still very close-knit family, and, given the state of transportation at the time, he had to assume that he would never see any of his brothers or sisters again once he left for the US. Moreover, had Selma not survived, Friedel's relationship with Frau Hansen might well have had a greater influence on his decision. None of my grandfather's siblings was very happy at the prospect of losing yet another brother (two Zins brothers had died fighting for Germany during the war), although most understood the need for Friedel and Selma to make a fresh start. Indeed, my grandfather's siblings did their best to put the alienation of the war years behind them. With *Oma* Maria no longer living, the big gatherings that had once been such a staple of Zins family life had grown uncommon, but when the time came for my grandparents to leave Frankfurt, Friedel's siblings organized a grand send-off.

The quest to get to America offered Friedel and Selma a welcome distraction from the strain in their marriage during those first few months back together. They began by re-establishing contact with Hermann and Rosi in New York, who agreed to act as their sponsors — if the US authorities would allow it. Once again, however, the couple had over-committed themselves. Still unsure whether any of their other family members had survived, Hermann and Rosi had already re-filed affidavits in support of their parents, as well as Bertha and her entire family. Fortunately, Friedel and Selma discovered another alternative.

In early 1946, with the US government perhaps feeling some remorse towards those it had earlier abandoned, President Harry S Truman issued an executive order establishing priority immigration status for up to 39,000 displaced and persecuted Europeans. My grandparents, because of Selma's time in Ravenbrück, qualified under the so-called Truman Initiative for their long-sought-after entry visas.

At about this same time, my grandmother's cousin, Heinz Baer, also wanted to come to America. In his case, however, Hermann, who was Heinz's first cousin, actively blocked the way — for reasons which became clear only many years later. Heinz, like Hermann's own father Berthold, had an inherited deformity of one hand, a condition that seemed to afflict only the males of the family. Hermann, along with other members of the Baer clan who had made it to America, had agreed never to acknowledge or discuss this "defect" in their bloodline. Assisting one of their own who carried the affliction would clearly have violated this secret pact.

It must never have occurred to Hermann and his fellow plotters just how chillingly their plan echoed the Nazis' own attempts to achieve genetic purity. What none of them understood was that the deformity they were so intent on screening out fell into a class of disorders known as "X-linked." This meant that while affected males could sire female carriers, they were incapable of passing the condition directly on to their own sons. This would have been obvious, even at that time, to anyone with a rudimentary knowledge of genetics. Had Hermann and his fellow plotters sought professional advice, they might well have avoided this whole sad chapter in their family history. As it was, Heinz Baer, who had survived years of incarceration at Theresienstadt, found himself barred by his closest remaining relatives from following them to freedom in America. Astonishingly, when the truth finally became known decades later, Cousin Heinz chose to forgive Hermann, allowing that "It was the best Hermann could do" under the circumstances.

Partly in response to the Truman Initiative, the American Joint Distribution Committee (JDC), a New York-based, private Jewish philanthropic organization, set up an office in Frankfurt to help Holocaust victims navigate the bureaucratic maze of the US immigration system. JDC also provided funds for the sea voyage and, for those like my grandparents who had no other means of support, worked to obtain corporate sponsorship from the National Refugee Service. That financial guarantee was the key that opened the door at last to a new life in the

United States for Friedel and Selma and their daughters.

As part of the required processing, the Zinses made several trips to the American Consulate in Frankfurt, where the four of them had to undergo thorough physical examinations. During one visit, American doctors discovered lice populating the heads of both girls. Even in the context of the postwar period, this provoked considerable embarrassment, especially for Erika. More importantly, the family would not be permitted to enter the country until they had eradicated the pests. Then as now, this required painstakingly picking through each strand of hair with a fine-toothed comb night after night for several weeks.

When the day of their departure came, my mother's family made their way to Frankfurt's main station and boarded a train bound for the northern port city of Bremen. The ship they were to sail on would be crowded, so each of them could bring along only 175 pounds of personal belongings. Everything else had to be left behind. Ironically, much of the clothing they owned had originally come only a short while earlier from America, sent to them by Hermann and Rosi when mail service resumed after the war.

When the train carrying my mother's family reached Bremen, they disembarked to find huge throngs of refugees already gathered there awaiting their chance to leave. It took another couple of days to complete the final processing, during which time they slept in a former Army barracks inside the city. During the day, immigration officials conducted orientation sessions, informing the new émigrés about how they would be met, what their initial housing arrangements would be, and the availability of job training after arrival. In the evenings, social events took the fore. These parties tended to be joyous affairs, and it was at the refugees' dance that first night after arriving in Bremen that Friedel taught his eldest daughter to waltz. Despite everything they had endured, my grandfather could never resist the chance to be dashing.

On the morning of the third day, the Zinses climbed into buses waiting to take them down to the harbor. My mother's family was part of the third large group of refugees to leave Germany under Truman's plan. At the pier, Friedel, Selma, and their girls joined the endless hoards making their way up the gangway to the S.S. *Marine Flasher*, a former merchant marine vessel. The boarding process took hours. As if the discomforts of the crowds and the delays weren't enough, my grandparents soon discovered that a few lucky refugees would be traveling in style. For reasons they never did figure out, a group of Jews from Poland had somehow secured first class accommodations, complete with white linen tablecloths adorning their dining tables during meals. Officials also allowed these pampered souls to bring along many more of their household goods. Friedel and Selma couldn't help feeling a little jealous during the boarding, as they watched workers loading crate after crate of the Polish passengers' possessions into the bowels of the ship.

At last, on the afternoon of June 6, 1946, the *Flasher* eased away from the dock and out into the North Sea. Passengers packed the deck in front of the huge American flag draped from the ship's bridge behind them. As the width of water between ship and pier widened, Erika heaved her last remaining German coins over the side and into the sea.

Accommodations on board turned out to be quite spartan. Men and women slept in separate holds with row upon row of bunks stacked three tiers high. To Selma, this must have seemed more than a little reminiscent of concentration camp life. For the girls, the hardest thing to get used to was the lack of doors on the toilets or showers, a remnant of the ship's previous life as a troop carrier. It was several days before the two adolescents could comfortably relieve themselves in such a public setting.

"Refugees aboard the SS Flasher *in Bremen (on the voyage prior to that of the Zins family)"*

What was not at all spartan was the food. Passengers took their meals together at long communal tables, most of them having never imagined such abundance. The cornucopia of fresh fruit, in particular, was something that none of the Europeans had ever seen before. Erika tasted her first grapefruit, an item not previously imported into Germany. Inge was fascinated by ketchup, another completely unfamiliar American staple. After the years of deprivation, many of the refugees gorged themselves those first few days at sea, with predictable results. Seasickness was rampant, but most of the passengers kept right on eating anyway.

JDC paid the full cost of $142 per adult (plus a $10 visa fee) for my grandparents to make the crossing. All told, the organization funded almost half of the *Flasher's* 822 passengers (589 displaced persons, plus an additional 233 returning Americans) at a total cost of nearly $34,000 (nearly ten times that amount in current dollars) for that sailing alone.

In addition, Joint Distribution gave each adult $5 in pocket money upon boarding and another $5 shortly before arrival in New York.

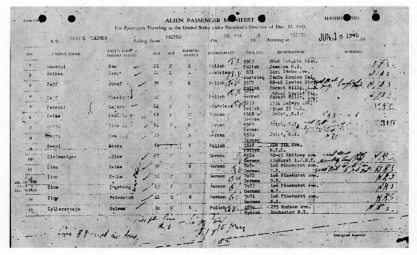

"Passenger manifest for the U.S.S. Flasher"

Most of those who sailed on the *Flasher* with my mother's family were fellow Germans, the rest were a mixture of Poles, Russians, Latvians, Yugoslavs, Czechs, and Romanians—a virtual smorgasbord of Nazi victims. Flags of each nation flew from poles arrayed on the main deck. Also among the passengers was a group of orphaned children ranging in age from nine months to eighteen years, though almost none were between six and twelve. That particular demographic slice—too young to do useful work but too old to have engendered mercy—had been exterminated with particular efficiency by Hitler's regime.

Life on board the *Flasher* was crowded, confined, and dull. A few of the refugees, unable to tolerate the sheer boredom of the long days at sea, volunteered for kitchen duty and other light chores around the ship, endearing themselves to the crew in the process. Others attempted to organize various activities for their fellow travelers. Several former performers put together their own impromptu cabaret. A group of orthodox Hungarian Jews held religious services for the Jewish holiday of *Shavuot*. For the most part, though, the refugees spent their idle hours sunning themselves on the main deck, chatting with fellow émigrés, or trying to decipher one of the English language books that crewmembers had brought along.

"Sunning on the deck of the Flasher (arrow indicates Erika)"

Very early on the morning of the twelfth day at sea, the captain's voice rang out over the ship's PA system, interrupting the overnight calm. All hands hurriedly gathered on deck and cast their eyes out over the rail as the *Flasher* glided through the entrance to New York Harbor. Like countless others before them, my grandparents' first glimpse of their new country was the sight of the Statue of Liberty, glinting in the light of a new dawn. Erika had seen pictures of the famous symbol when she was in school, but now, gazing at the Lady of Freedom for the first time, the Zinses could at last allow themselves to hope that their worst experiences were behind them. US Immigration officers boarded the ship to complete the last formalities, and a short time later, my mother's family strode down the gangplank into the waiting arms of Hermann and Rosi, now accompanied by their young son Steven — the first in the family to have been born in the New World.

"Refugee children arriving in NY Harbor"

There was little time to waste. JDC provided no ongoing support, so like most other new immigrants Friedel and Selma went to work immediately in factories around New York City. After battling for so long just to get to the US, my grandparents had no chance to relax in their adopted country. And there were other problems, too. Selma was still suffering from bouts of anxiety and depression. The psychological wounds she had sustained in the camp would not heal completely for decades. She consulted a variety of practitioners, searching in vain for some measure of relief.

In the mid-1950s, my grandparents filed for restitution under a program established by new German government, but they erred fatally in their choice of an advocate. Reading through their correspondence of the time, it's clear that Selma's German lawyer was ambivalent about her claim, very likely due to his own lingering anti-Semitism. He failed to enthusiastically push their case, and as a result, German officials denied Selma's request, concluding that her problems were unrelated to her concentration camp experiences.

My grandfather had his own issues to work out. Though now an ocean away, he could not break his emotional attachment to his former mistress. Things got so bad between my grandparents that at one point Friedel even made plans to take Erika and return to Germany permanently. Fortunately, before he could follow through, he received an urgent message from one of his nieces, who reported seeing her neighbor, Frau Hansen, hanging her stained menstrual garments on the clothesline between their apartments. Exposing the fabricated claim of pregnancy did finally sever the link, allowing my grandparents to focus their energies on reconciling their own relationship and succeeding together in their new lives in America.

At work, Friedel strained to grasp the change to English measurements. One day, a co-worker told him of a job opening as superintendent of a nearby apartment building. Friedel jumped at the opportunity to escape the factory. He was attracted as well by the free apartment that came with the job. In the tight postwar housing market, the move boosted the family's standard of living to a level they could not have otherwise hoped to achieve. Selma remained on the assembly line until her daughters were grown and out of the house. Then, with fewer mouths to feed, she quit working for good. It was her first extended respite since returning from the camps years before, and my grandmother relished the freedom to stay at home and run their simple household.

*"A Tender Moment — Friedel and Selma in the
early years after their arrival in America"*

Erika and Inge acclimated quickly to American life. Despite having not a word of English when they landed, my mother and her sister soon learned to speak the language without the slightest hint of an accent. The family needed their income, so college was not an option. Instead, both girls went to trade school and became hairdressers. As they entered adulthood, the two sisters embraced their own versions of the American dream, marrying up-and-coming young university graduates and raising families amidst the relative affluence of middle class America. For Erika and Inge Zins, working-class refugees from Hitler's Germany, this was a level of comfort and success that they could not have dreamed of amidst the chaos of war just a few short years before.

"Erika" and "Inge"

Hermann and Rosi were the first of the immigrant generation to escape the confines of the city, buying a home in suburban New Jersey where they raised their only son. Although Friedel and Selma continued to visit the Baers often, an unmistakable coolness persisted between my grandfather and his brother-in-law. After those first couple of weeks in country, Hermann had presented Friedel with a bill for some seventy-odd dollars in incidental expenses, expecting to be reimbursed. After all my grandparents had been through, and all he had done to help Hermann and Rosi — especially during the *Kristallnacht* — Friedel could never forgive what felt to him like a betrayal.

In the mid-1960s, my grandparents returned to Frankfurt for the first time. For Friedel, it had been almost twenty years since he had seen his siblings. Selma would have been just as happy never to go back to Germany, but she went along anyway, knowing how important the trip was to her husband. When the two of them landed at the airport, the whole extended Zins clan was there to greet them. The stress and alienation of the war years had faded into the past, and all had been forgiven. No one seemed interested in re-opening old wounds.

After their retirement, my grandparents moved into Inge's home near Washington, D.C. There, comfortably ensconced in their own small apartment, the two of them spent many happy years entertaining their growing hoard of adoring grandchildren. Their marriage, so strained at one point in their lives, continued to strengthen as they grew older — so much so that those of us who grew up watching them would find their unique bond worthy of emulating.

"Friedel and Selma — growing older"

Why Selma forgave her husband for his earlier infidelity is hard to say for sure, but I think it echoes a choice that all survivors had to make. What had happened to Hitler's victims, as unspeakably horrible as it was, could never again be undone. Every survivor I've ever talked to has had to make the conscious decision to let go of his or her anger over the unfairness of it all in order to build a new life. Dwelling on the past was a sure path only to bitterness, and although she never talked to me about it, I'm sure my grandmother must ultimately have come to this realization.

In their later years, it was Selma who succumbed first to the infirmities of age. The day Friedel gave her up to the nursing home, his spirit was broken. The memory of that promise he had made on a street corner across from the burning building in Frankfurt long ago reverberated in his conscience, and he never forgave himself. My grandmother died in December of 1984. Less than a year later, he was gone too — but not before the two of them had had the chance to share their stories, and their way of life, with a brand new generation.

Sixty years later, my mother can still conjure up the vision of the first night she spent in America. The four of them clambered up to the roof of the Baer's apartment building in Washington Heights. As they gazed out over the city, the images of blacked-out Frankfurt still fresh in their minds, the endless twinkling sea of New York's lights sparked a vision of freedom in the immigrants' new land.

EPILOGUE:
A CODE TO LIVE BY

Only six months to go. It'd taken me nine years since I'd left home to get through college and medical school, and three more after that to complete my residency. Just a few more weeks, and at age thirty, I'd finally be earning my first real paycheck.

The head of my training program was a tall, soft-spoken man who seemed to move in perpetual slow motion. He took his role as a teacher of new physicians seriously, probably a little bit too seriously. That much had been clear from the beginning. The director had spent the past few months lobbying the hospital's CEO to buy him a new video monitoring system, which he intended to install in each of the exam rooms of the clinic the hospital had built for him the year before. The idea was to tape patient encounters for analysis afterwards with faculty members. I have to admit it was an effective teaching technique. I'll never forget the time I watched myself talking to one of my favorite elderly patients about his long list of problems and what we were going to do about them. I was so proud of my plan, which had demanded every bit of skill I had as a physician to construct. It had been a strenuous mental exercise, but it felt good to work so hard for a patient I really connected with, or so I thought. As I observed our discussion later on tape, I saw the old man's eyes glaze over after item #2 on my list. Why had I not noticed that before? It had never occurred to me while I was in the room that if the plan were so complicated for me to put together, this poor fellow would have no chance to understand it, much less to follow through on all my recommendations.

There was a lot about the taping program that made me itch, however. Before going live, we had asked each patient to sign a blanket consent form, granting permission to record any future encounter for educational purposes. The vast majority of our mostly poor and under-educated population, grateful for a place to go for care that wouldn't turn them away, signed without a second thought. We filed the forms in the back of their charts and everybody forgot about them.

I tried not to think too hard about the issue of just how freely consent had been given, until one day when I conducted a routine annual physical for a young woman. We chatted for a while about what had been going on in her life and I took her through the standard part of the exam. Excusing myself for a moment, I then had the nurse prepare her for her pelvic exam, which went without incident.

Later on, as I sat with a faculty member and several of my fellow trainees and watched the film of my interaction with this woman, I knew something just wasn't right. I tried to explain my discomfort to my colleagues, to no avail. At the very least, I said, we should ask patients to give their consent each time we're going to tape them, especially in such sensitive situations. Not possible, was the instantaneous reply. If we reminded patients, it might skew the whole encounter and a valuable teaching opportunity would be lost.

That just wasn't good enough. The whole thing felt so deceptive that I just couldn't keep working like that. If my superiors wouldn't relent, I'd have to take action myself. Before my next clinic session, I unplugged the cameras in my exam rooms.

A day or two afterward, the director found out what I had done. He had his secretary page me to his office. *Great*, I thought, *all grown up and summoned to the principal's office.* When I got there, the man's usual mild-mannered demeanor had disappeared. This had been his pet project and he was livid.

"Close the door," he commanded. "Sit down."

I lowered myself into the chair, hoping he wouldn't notice the vise grip I had on the armrests, and tried to disguise the annoying little tremor that seemed to have taken over the upper half of my body. I glanced around at the walls of the room, which seemed to have receded a remarkable distance, leaving the two of us in the middle of the void staring at each other. I had the sense that his four angelic-looking children were watching us from their photos arrayed on either side of an otherwise spotless expanse of desk.

"You had no right to take apart those cameras," the director went on, his face instantaneously darkening to an alarming crimson as he warmed to his task.

What right did I need? I remember thinking.

"I should fire you right now," he threatened. "Get back out there, do your job, and don't you even think about pulling a stunt like this again," he barked. End of conversation. With no chance to defend myself, I backed out of the room and the confrontation was over.

Had I been dismissed, it would have meant repeating the last two years of training in another program in some other city, assuming I could even find another residency director willing to take me on with such a history. I don't recall thinking about the possibility of being fired before disabling those cameras, but it wouldn't have made any difference if I had. What I do remember, clearly, is asking myself what my grandfather would have done in that situation.

There have been other instances, too, where my grandparents' example has guided me, one of which occurs almost every time I go to work. In my job as an ER physician, I often see patients wanting narcotic prescriptions for their pain. Some of these requests are legitimate, from patients with cancer or other serious illnesses, but many of them are not. Some seek the drugs to mask their emotional pain, others are simply addicted but refuse to admit it, and more than a few are trying to score a supply they can sell on the street. It can be difficult to say no, as refusal often sparks a formal complaint to the hospital administration, usually couched in terms of "unprofessional behavior." Given our consumerist culture, the higher-ups assume that the patients are always right. Doctors are viewed as guilty until proven innocent.

Some of my colleagues have chosen not to fight this battle and prescribe more freely. I can't criticize them for this — the pressure to concede is relentless — but I cannot practice that way. Inevitably then, I spend a lot of effort defending my actions to hospital administrators, and at least on one occasion I've lost a job I really liked because of it. It's a price I am willing to pay.

Even now, more than twenty years after their deaths, there are days when I still feel my grandparents' loss acutely. In the process of researching and writing about their lives, I've thought a great deal about what it was that enabled them to live through the Nazi threat when so many others did not. The truth is that there is no real answer to that question. No doubt luck played a big part, whether in the form of sympathetic, non-informing neighbors, or through the unwitting protection gained from Selma's religious conversion and the children's baptisms — a fortunate consequence of actions taken for very different reasons.

Every survivor I've ever talked to has been quick to point out that strength of character alone was not enough. Many others, equally as determined as my grandparents, nevertheless lost their lives. Still, I'm certain that their story contains a lesson worthy of emulating. In spite of the fear and danger they lived through, Friedel and Selma never jettisoned their sense of right from wrong. Though they had ample reason for doing so, neither of them permitted the extreme circumstances to seduce them into acting in ways inconsistent with the type of people they believed themselves to be. The same is undoubtedly true of most others who have experienced the traumas of wars before and since, and yet returned to integrate themselves successfully back into their former lives. This ability, to somehow set aside what cannot be changed, however horrible, is in my opinion the defining characteristic of Holocaust survivors who have found peace in their reconstructed lives. It explains how Selma was ultimately able to forgive her husband's infidelity, and indeed, to look past her experiences in the camp and go on with the rest of her life. I'm convinced that such fortitude and integrity are rare enough to warrant preserving as a birthright to future generations of our family.

Friedel and Selma's "secret" is really quite simple then, and it was there for me to see even as a young boy. It just took me until now to understand it. Adopt a code of ethics to live by, and apply those standards day in and day out, especially to all the little things that happen in life. Then, when the big challenges come along, you'll know instinctively what the right thing to do is. I learned from my grandparents that strength of conviction, practiced over a lifetime, will supply the courage needed to act. I'd like to think that I live my life by that principle. I know I try to. Thanks, Nanny and Poppop, for showing me the way.

ACKNOWLEDGMENTS

Over the past decade, in the course of bringing the story of my grandparents' lives to print, I have had the good fortune to work with a great number of interesting and talented people. Along the way, I've tried to express to each of them how grateful I am for their contributions to a project so close to my heart.

Two individuals deserve the lion's share of the thanks. The first is my mother, Erika Lake, who traveled with me on every step of this adventure and whose stories and insights provided much of the material that forms the basis for this book. The other is my cousin, Doris Hugo, a talented and indefatigable researcher. Without Doris' unrelenting pursuit of trails long since gone cold, I would not have been able to tell this tale.

Several other individuals deserve special mention, including Frau Erna de Vries of Lathen, Germany, and Dr. Margrit Wreschner-Rustow, now residing in New York City. Each of these survivors of Ravensbrück spent many hours helping me to understand firsthand what my grandmother's concentration camp experience must have been like. No less important was Christa Bauer of Ifta, who held me spellbound one afternoon as she filled in the details of my grandmother's escape from the Soviet zone, and then took me to the spot where her grandfather had risked his own freedom so that a woman he barely knew could go home at last. Finally, there is my writing coach and mentor, Charisse Coleman. In my initial attempts, I somehow managed to turn my grandparents' dramatic exploits into a boring historical account. If what you are about to read succeeds in holding your interest, or perhaps even inspires you in some small way, Charisse deserves a great deal of the credit for that.

No project of this scope can succeed without help on the home front. The ten-plus years I spent researching and writing this book coincided with an otherwise very busy time in my life. In the midst of raising three small children and pursuing a full-time career in medicine, I got to fly off periodically to Europe and elsewhere, while my wife Susan stayed behind without complaint. Without her constant support, none of this would have been possible. I hope someday to be able to take her to the fascinating places I have seen.

A Note on Sources
And Methods

This book originally grew out of interviews I conducted with my mother between 1995 and 2001. At the time, my intent was just to preserve on tape the tales I had heard as a young boy, before all those with first-hand memory of the events of WWII passed from the scene.

After visiting Ravensbrück for the first time, my mother and I stopped in Frankfurt on the way home to visit with my grandfather's relatives. We were sitting around the table one day, drinking coffee with her first cousin Doris Hugo (granddaughter to Friedel's sister Hannah), when we got to talking about the reasons for our trip. Though not formally educated as a researcher, Doris and her husband had spent several years traveling to the Republic of Ireland to indulge their interest in that country's turbulent history. It turned out that Doris was also quite interested in her own country's recent past, and she asked if there was any way she could help with my project.

I had no idea what was out there. But as a native speaker, and with her remarkable sense of where to look in the vast and often impenetrable German bureaucracy, Doris uncovered document after document that both corroborated my grandparents' stories and filled in the details of their wartime experiences. To this day, I am amazed by the plethora of written material that still exists from that period, more than half a century after the Nazis' determined efforts to destroy the evidence of their crimes. One only has to know where to look, and to refuse to ever take no for an answer. Doris does this better than anyone else I know.

Among her other finds, it was Doris who discovered my grandmother's six-page hand written account of life in the concentration camp, prepared in the early 1950s as part of her claim for reparations and long since stuffed away in a file cabinet in some obscure German agency in Wiesbaden. It was Doris, too, whose diligence in tracking down every last detail led to the eventual discovery of the collection of forgotten letters from my great grandmother — a unique and chilling reincarnation of Jenny Baer's own voice from inside Nazi Germany. And, it was Doris who found Christa Bauer and arranged our visit to Ifta, perhaps the single most stunning moment in this entire journey. It is no exaggeration to say that without the years of hard work on the part of Doris Hugo, Friedel and Selma's story would not have survived beyond living memory.

Along the way, I've also interviewed other family members who lived through WWII Frankfurt, each of whom provided me with their own differing perspective on those events. Most notable among these were my great aunt, Rosi Baer, still active and lucid well into her nineties; my mother's sister Inge, whose own memories turned out to be much hazier than those of her older sibling; and Robert Zins, son of Friedel's steadfastly-loyal older brother Heinrich, who just a few weeks before his death provided me with fascinating details about the attitudes of the rest of the Zins brothers and sisters towards their tainted sibling.

I've tried to weave into these first-person accounts historical information gleaned from a variety of other sources, both published and unpublished. Most notable among these were Monika Kingreen's *Nach der Kristallnacht*, the most comprehensive accounting of the Jewish experience in Frankfurt during WWII; Katharina Katzenmeier's *Vom KZ ins Kloster*, described earlier in the chapter on Ravensbrück; and Valentin Senger's *Kaiserhofstrasse 12*, about the life of a Russian-Jewish immigrant living under-the-radar in Nazi-era Frankfurt.

Finally, I wish to remind the reader that this is intended to be a work of creative non-fiction. Despite the plethora of sources, there are instances, especially with regards to my grandparents' thoughts and motives, where I simply do not have verifiable first-hand accounts to guide the narrative. In these cases, I have relied upon my own knowledge of their personalities to imagine what might have been going through their minds at the time. In all such cases, I've chosen language to clearly label my speculations and inferences for what they are. Ultimately, it is for those of you who peruse this account to decide how faithful I have been to the character of these two extraordinary people.

APPENDIX A

Family Tree of Friedrich Ludwig Zins

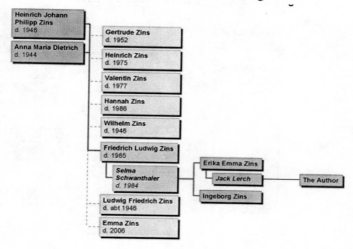

Family Tree of Selma Schwanthaler Zins

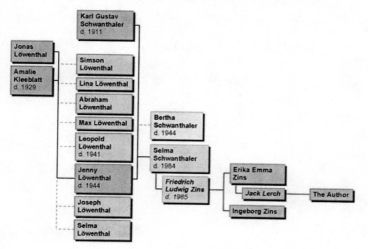

Family Tree of Jenny Löwenthal Baer

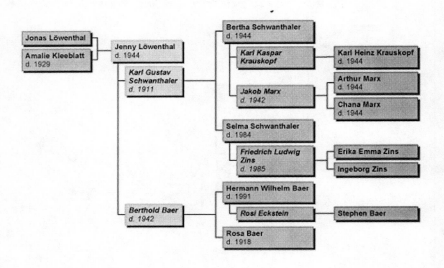

APPENDIX B

Map of WWII Europe

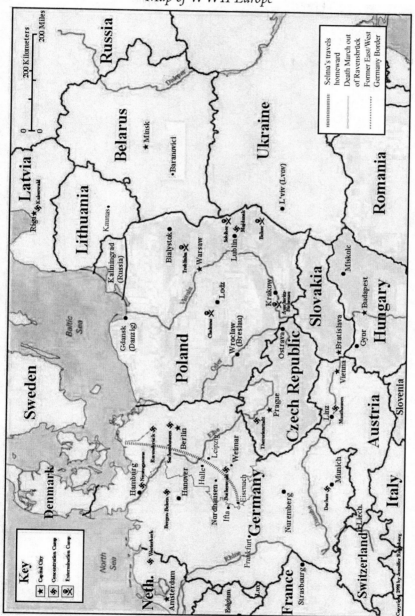

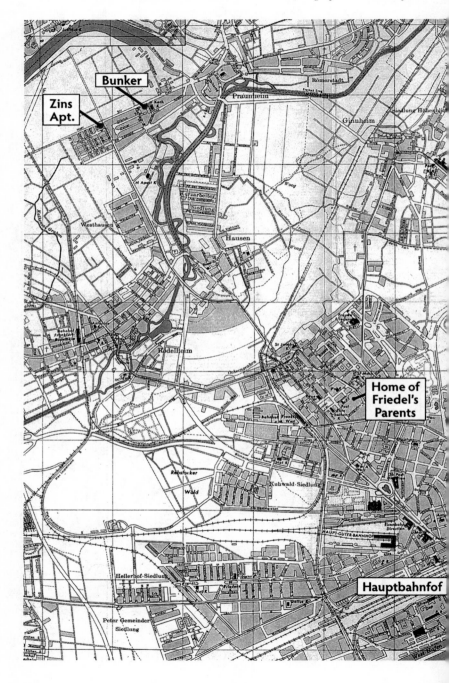

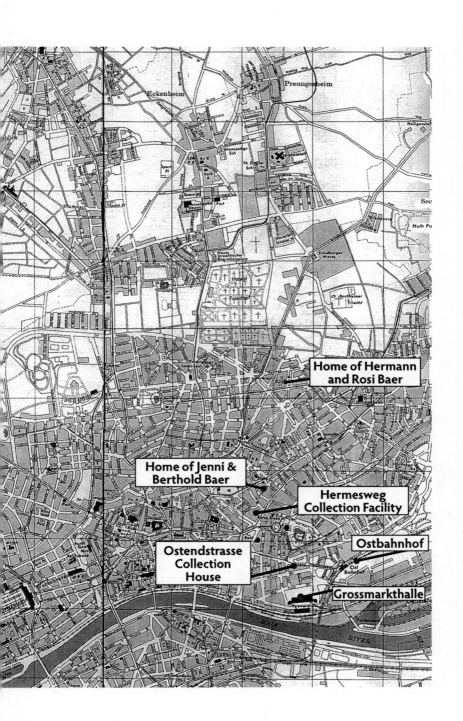

Preungesheim

Eckenheim

Home of Hermann
and Rosi Baer

Home of Jenni &
Berthold Baer

Hermesweg
Collection Facility

Ostendstrasse
Collection
House

Ostbahnhof

Grossmarkthalle

SELECTED
BIBLIOGRAPHY

Bernstein, Sara T. *The Seamstress.* New York: G.P. Putnam's Sons, 1997. (Well-written and readable description of life inside Ravensbrück. Also includes heart-rending account of how the Nazis destroyed a Romanian Jewish community that had existed for centuries.

Browning, Christopher R. *The Origins of the Final Solution: The Evolution of Nazi Jewish Policy*, September 1939-1942. Lincoln, Nebraska: University of Nebraska Press, 2004. (Comprehensive explanation of Nazi regime's policies towards its Jewish victims.)

Czech, Danuta. *Auschwitz Chronicle.* New York: Henry Holt and Company, 1990. (Day-by-day history of events at the Auschwitz extermination camp.)

Feldenkirchen, Wilfried. *Siemens 1918-1945.* Munich: R. Piper GmbH, 1995. (Company-promoted account of its history. Contains short passage describing operations at Ravensbrück.)

Füllberg-Stolberg, Claus, et al. *Frauen in Konzentrationslagern: Bergen-Belsen/Ravensbrück* (in German). Bremen, Germany: Edition Temmen 1994. (Textbook with chapters detailing various aspects of life in the camps.)

Heppner, Ernest G. *Shanghai Refuge.* Lincoln, Nebraska: University of Nebraska Press, 2003. (First-hand account of the German-Jewish refugee experience in China.)

Katzenmaier, Katharina. *Vom KZ ins Kloster* (in German). St. Ottilien,

Germany: EOS-Verlag, 1996. (First person account of life in Ravens-brück and during the subsequent Death March by traveling companion of Selma Zins.)

Kingreen, Monika (Ed.). *Nach der Kristallnacht: Jüdisches Leben und antijüdisches Politik in Frankfurt am Main 1938-1945* (in German). Frankfurt: Campus Verlag, 1999. (Thorough account from variety of experts describing the experience of Frankfurt Jews during the Nazi years.)

Klemperer, Victor. *I Will Bear Witness: A Diary of the Nazi Years 1933-1945* (2 vols.). New York: Random House, 1988. (Diary of life in Berlin during the Nazi years, written by former Professor of Romance Languages who was forced from his position by Hitler's regime but remained protected by his marriage to a non-Jew.)

Lundholm, Anja. *Das Höllentor* (in German). Hamburg: Rowohlt Verlag, 1988. (Perhaps the most detailed, and most harrowing, of the many survivor accounts of Ravensbrück.)

Morrison, Jack G. *Ravensbrück: Everyday Life in a Women's Concentration Camp 1939-1945.* Princeton, NJ: Markus Wiener Publishers, 2000. (English-language account by US historian detailing various aspects of camp life.)

Philipp, Grit. *Kalendarium: der Ereignisse im Frauen-Konzentrationslager Ravensbrück* (in German). Berlin: Metropol Verlag, 1999. (Day-to-day history of events at the Ravensbrück work camp.)

Senger, Valentin. *Kaiserhofstraße 12* (in German). Frankfurt: Büchergilde Gutenberg, 1979. (Fascinating account of life under-the-radar by Russian Jewish émigré to Frankfurt.)

75 Jahre May-Siedlung Praunheim 1927-2002 (in German). Frankfurt: Siedlungverein Frankfurt am Main — Praunheim e.V., 2002. (History of the Praunheim neighborhood.)

Stoltzfus, Nathan. *Resistance of the Heart.* New Brunswick, NJ: Rutgers University Press, 1996. (Account of the only known successful mass protest against Nazi policies within Germany. Also contains interesting details of the threats that confronted mixed-religious couples.)

Tennenbaum, Silvia. *Yesterday's Streets.* New York: Random House, 1981. (Fictionalized account of Jewish life in Frankfurt during the early 20th century based on author's own first-person experience.)

Theresienstädter Gedenkbuch: die Opfer der Judentransporte aus Deutschland nach Theresienstadt 1942-1945. Prague: Institut Theresienstädter Initiative, 2000. (Listing of the fate of each of the victims of the Theresienstadt camp, organized by city of origin.)

Photo Credits

211

Page	Title	Source
115	*Karl Heinz Krauskopf and his little brother*	Erika Lake collection
118	*Tranquil vista*	Author's collection
123	*Entrance to Ravensbrück*	Author's collection
124	*Twelve foot high walls*	Author's collection
131	*Appell grounds*	Author's collection
133	*Area of former Siemens camp*	Author's collection
140	*Author (center) with mother, siblings...*	Author's collection
142	*Friedel and his girls*	Erika Lake collection
154	*Christa Bauer (center)*	Author's collection
160	*The Hotel Zur Tanne*	unknown
161	*The Wartburg-Klinikum*	Wartburg Klinikum, Eisenach
163	*Wartburg-Klinikum register*	Wartburg Klinikum, Eisenach
165	*Paula Busch Kutscher*	courtesy Ursula Burghardt
166	*Berthold Busch*	Christa Bauer collection
166	*The Mistwagen*	Christa Bauer collection
167	*Edge of Busch family land today*	Author's collection
169	*The Wheels*	Author's collection
181	*Refugees aboard the SS Flasher*	AJDC archives
182	*Passenger manifest for the USS Flasher*	US National Archives, Washington, D.C.
183	*Sunning on the deck...*	Erika Lake collection
184	*Refugee children arriving ...*	from photo in AJDC hqtrs
186	*A Tender Moment*	Erika Lake collection
187	*Erika and Inge*	Erika Lake collection
188	*Friedel and Selma - growing older*	Erika Lake collection
203	*Map of WWII Europe*	adapted from map, copyright: Jennifer Rosenberg
204	*Map of 1940's Frankfurt*	SUNY Buffalo library collection

ABOUT THE AUTHOR

Victor Lerch, M.D. lives in North Carolina with his wife of twenty-five years and their three teenage children. Dr. Lerch began his writing career in the late 1990s penning opinion pieces for *The News and Observer* (of Raleigh) on the state of the healthcare crisis in America. His full-time job as an ER physician has also provided a steady stream of human interest stories that have appeared as essays in medical journals and other publications. *Four Wheels to Freedom*, the author's first book-length work, represents the culmination of nearly ten years of research and writing. A collection of Dr. Lerch's writings can be found at **www.fourwheelstofreedom.com**. Signed copies of this book may be ordered by e-mailing the author directly at **info@ fourwheelstofreedom.com**.

LaVergne, TN USA
08 October 2010
200094LV00003B/4/P

9 780979 888717